Writing In Narrative

The acronym *WIN*, the phrase *Writing in Narrative* and all titles in the *WIN - Writing in Narrative* series are copyrighted. No part of any book in the series may be duplicated by any means with the exception of the template pages. These pages are meant to be filled in by the student and may be duplicated if additional pages are needed for the *exclusive* use of the purchaser.

WIN - Writing in Narrative: Story Writing, The Four Parts of a Story
By Peter Joel and Dr. Leslie Simonson
First edition © 1990
This edition © 1996 ISBN 1-884098-06-1

The Elijah Company
Route 2 Box 100B
Crossville, TN 38555-9600
Phone 615/456-6284
Fax 615/456-6384
E-mail elijahco@midtenn.net

Writing In Narrative—The "WIN" Program
Scope and Sequence

Book A: Story Writing by Dictation. A Three-Step Introduction
to the WIN Program
(Grades: K-1 — saddle stitched)

This Teacher/Parent/Student Edition is designed to provide kindergarten and first grade students—whose writing language skills are not yet developed—with a means for creating and expressing simple stories in a **logical** format. *Story Writing By Dictation* begins to familiarize students with the meaning of each of the four story parts. *Story Writing by Dictation* will prepare students for a more formal introduction to story writing procedures found in the succeeding levels.

Book I: The Seven Sentence Story; A Simplified Introduction to Story
Writing
(Grades: Primary — saddle stitched)

This Teacher/Parent/Student Edition formally introduces students to the four major story parts: Setting, Problem, Solution, and Conclusion. The book also illustrates **logical** sequence in a story and uses the Four-Boxed Story Form to facilitate the students' understanding of paragraphing. In addition, *The Seven Sentence Story* is intended to prepare students for an in-depth presentation of the major story parts and sub-skills found in the *WIN Book II*. Moreover, the *Seven Sentence Story* may be considered a short **introduction** to the entire WIN Program as presented in *WIN Book II* & *WIN Book III* (see below). However, it is not necessary to use *The Seven Sentence Story* prior to using *WIN Book II*, because *WIN Book II* contains in expanded form the material found in *The Seven Sentence Story*. *The Seven Sentence Story* is a good place to introduce creative writing to the beginning writer.

Book II: Writing in Narrative; Story Writing: The Four Parts of a Story
(Grades: 3-7+ comb bound)

This Teacher/Parent/Student Edition expands on the information presented in *The Seven Sentence Story* while providing more information about the major story parts: adding new sub-parts, introducing the "Pre-Story Writing Outline," and presenting material involving capitalization, punctuation, dialogue, and synonyms. *WIN Book II* also introduces stories with a **Goal**, or **Challenge**, in place of a Problem.

Book III: Writing in Narrative; Enriched Story Writing:
Adding the Fifth Paragraph
(Grades: 6-Senior High — comb bound)

This Teacher/Parent/Student Edition continues the orderly development of story writing skills by adding a fifth major paragraph. Also included are lessons in descriptive writing, summarizing stories, basic research and reporting, short mystery stories, and journal story writing. Finally, *WIN Book III* introduces advanced writing techniques through the use of descriptive elements, such as color, shape, design, light, shadow, texture, and scent.

ACKNOWLEDGMENTS

The authors wish to express their grateful appreciation to Patty Irving for her typing and editorial assistance in the development of the "WIN" program.

A debt of appreciation is also due Loren Grossi for his faith in this program.

Thanks is also due Al Nubling for offering helpful suggestions regarding this project.

In addition, a very special thanks is due Pat Langley for the generous sharing of her editorial talents and for her unique insights into how students learn.

AUTHORS' PERSPECTIVE

Teaching students to write well is instilling a habit of mind. Writing well is more than just writing regularly. It is instilling the value in knowing the inexactitudes of human thought and the necessity to correct them. Therefore, a good writing program establishes procedures that gradually train students to have precise habits of thought. The "WIN" program encompasses not only a sequence of lessons designed to teach story writing and related writing skills, but it also includes learning components designed to instill the habit of careful analysis that leads to fine story writing.

INTRODUCTION TO THE "WIN" LEVEL II PROGRAM

The "WIN" story writing program remained formally untitled for a period of many months following its introduction into the authors' (Joel and Simonson) third grade classrooms in the fall of 1986. Then, the superior writing achievement of the "WIN" third graders (as validated by the authors' school district testing) furnished objective verification of the effectiveness of the WIN Program. Furthermore, after analyzing the 1988 test results, Joel and Simonson concluded that WIN students saw themselves as "WINNERS" in story writing. Hence, in an attempt to capture the "winning" enthusiasm and confidence which the program had instilled in their students, the authors entitled their program "WIN" (**W**riting **I**n **N**arrative).

Although the Level II WIN Program has been targeted for the third, fourth, and fifth grades, it has also been used successfully with junior high and high school students. The format of the program allows the teacher and student (third grade or higher) to communicate comfortably and clearly when discussing a story's strengths and weaknesses. Unlike other writing programs reviewed by the authors, WIN provides **an explanation of the major sections of a story** (Setting, Story Problem Action-Solution, and Conclusion), the **components of each of these sections,** and **the names used to identify the major sections and their respective components.** Therefore, the teacher or student can easily explain which story parts, if any, are either missing or lacking sufficient detail or development.

The actual foundation of the WIN Program consists of model stories and related lesson sheets. The lesson sheets allow students to work on one section of a story at a time. Thus, students can develop their story writing skills on a regular basis **without** having to concentrate their attention on completing a story in a single class period. In other words, this format means that stories are written in a developmental, step-by-step process. Consequently, children not only grasp the logical structure of a story, but they also develop their own **individual** writing styles. They learn to select details that give story sections a feeling of excitement, humor, adventure, or a combination of these qualities.

In order to facilitate the students' understanding of the logical structure of a story, Joel and Simonson have incorporated into the WIN Program a unique feature known as "Connecting Sentences." Students learn that these sentences, which are summary-like in nature, create a framework around which the rest of a story expands. In addition, students learn that Connecting Sentences function as transitions between paragraphs by serving as signals to the writer that a change in the development of the story is occurring and that new events will be unfolding.

An example of the framework function of Connecting Sentences (in bold print below) and how a story would expand around them can be understood most easily by reading the following Connecting Sentences:

STARTING EVENT SENTENCE (Found in Setting Paragraph)

We were going on a balloon ride.

STORY PROBLEM SENTENCE (Found in Story Problem Paragraph)

We were going to crash!

SOLVING SENTENCE (Found in Action-Solution Paragraph)

The wind lifted the balloon over the cliff and saved us.

WHAT-WAS-LEARNED-SENTENCE (Found in Conclusion Paragraph)

I told my mom that I didn't want to ever go on a balloon ride again.

By using lesson learning sheets designed to familiarize students with Connecting Sentences and their placement in the major paragraphs, students learn to write stories in a logical, coherent fashion. This framework enables students to give more attention to descriptive writing and details that bring richness to a story.

Along with the lessons already described, Level II WIN also emphasizes the integration of a variety of other language skills with the story writing process. Such skills include punctuation, capitalization, use of varying sentence types, conversation, synonym usage, comparative analysis of functionally similar paragraphs, beginning outlining, and editing. These skills should be taught and used regularly in the students' story writing.

Perhaps the most striking characteristic of the WIN Program at all levels is its "user friendly" nature. No special training is needed for its implementation, and the teacher and student use the same book at a given level. (There are four WIN books plus an Essay Handbook.) Simply put, the student's grasp of the orderly design of the WIN format gives them a sense of the command in story writing. That is, they learn the value of organizing their thoughts logically as well as developing their creativity. In fact, the use of logic may be the single most important skill to be mastered in education. For this reason, the authors continue the orderly approach to story writing in the next book, *Level III WIN: Enriched Story Writing.*

TABLE OF CONTENTS

Acknowledgments.. iii

Authors' Perspective... iv

Introduction to the "WIN" Level II Program... v

Table of Contents.. vii

Suggestions to Teacher and Students... ix

LESSON 1: THE FOUR PARAGRAPHS OF A STORY.. 1

LESSON 2: PARTS OF THE PARAGRAPH.. 6

LESSON 3: CONNECTING SENTENCES.. 11

LESSON 4: INTRODUCTION OF SETTING PARAGRAPH PARTS........................ 16

LESSON 5: DISCUSSION OF SETTING PARAGRAPH PARTS............................. 20

LESSON 6: IDENTIFYING PARTS OF THE SETTING PARAGRAPH.................... 22

LESSON 7: WRITING A PRACTICE SETTING PARAGRAPH............................... 26

LESSON 8: DECISION TIME: DIRECTIONS AND ANSWER SHEET.................... 30

LESSON 9: INTRODUCTION OF STORY PROBLEM PARAGRAPH...................... 32

LESSON 10: DISCUSSION OF STORY PROBLEM PARAGRAPH.......................... 35

LESSON 11: IDENTIFYING PARTS OF THE STORY PROBLEM
PARAGRAPH.. 37

LESSON 12: WRITING A PRACTICE STORY PROBLEM PARAGRAPH................ 41

LESSON 13: DECISION TIME: DIRECTIONS AND ANSWER SHEET.................. 45

LESSON 14: INTRODUCTION OF ACTION-SOLUTION PARAGRAPH.................. 47

LESSON 15: DISCUSSION OF ACTION-SOLUTION PARAGRAPH....................... 50

LESSON 16: IDENTIFYING PARTS OF THE ACTION-SOLUTION
PARAGRAPH.. 52

LESSON 17: WRITING A PRACTICE ACTION-SOLUTION
PARAGRAPH.. 56

LESSON 18: DECISION TIME: DIRECTIONS AND ANSWER SHEET.................. 60

LESSON 19: INTRODUCTION OF CONCLUSION PARAGRAPH.................................. 62

LESSON 20: DISCUSSION OF CONCLUSION PARAGRAPH................................... 64

LESSON 21: IDENTIFYING PARTS OF THE CONCLUSION
PARAGRAPH.. 66

LESSON 22: WRITING A PRACTICE CONCLUSION PARAGRAPH.......................... 70

LESSON 23: DECISION TIME: DIRECTIONS AND ANSWER SHEET.................... 75

LESSON 24: WRITING A SETTING PARAGRAPH... 77

LESSON 25: WRITING A STORY PROBLEM PARAGRAPH.................................... 80

LESSON 26: WRITING AN ACTION-SOLUTION PARAGRAPH............................... 83

LESSON 27: WRITING A CONCLUSION PARAGRAPH.. 86

LESSON 28: STORY WRITING LESSON: AN EXCITING
ADVENTURE... 89

LESSON 29: STORIES WITHOUT A PROBLEM BUT WITH A GOAL.................... 95

LESSON 30: WRITING A STORY WITH A GOAL.. 101

APPENDICES... 106

APPENDIX A: STORY EXPANSION: USING STORY PROBLEM
FORMAT... A-1

APPENDIX B: DECISION TIME ANSWERS.. B-1

APPENDIX C: CAPITALIZATION AND PUNCTUATION...................................... C-1

APPENDIX D: QUOTATION MARKS AND CONVERSATION................................ D-1

APPENDIX E: SENTENCE STARTERS AND COMPOUND
SENTENCES... E-1

APPENDIX F: MODEL STORY CHARTS.. F-1

APPENDIX G: SPECIAL WORD LISTS.. G-1

APPENDIX H: STORY EDITING CHART.. H-1

APPENDIX I: STORY FORMS... I-1

APPENDIX J: STORY IDEAS.. J-1

APPENDIX K: PRE-STORY WRITING OUTLINE... K-1

SUGGESTIONS TO TEACHERS AND STUDENTS

TO THE TEACHER:

The WIN Level II Program gives students a four-part framework for building a story. Using this framework, students can start with simple stories of seven or eight sentences and gradually learn to add descriptive language, details, and connecting sentences to expand their stories and make them more interesting.

The actual work of creating a story is accomplished through having the students examine sample stories and then fill in "Story Charts." Lessons 1 through 22 have instructions addressed to both the teacher and the student. Instructions in Lessons 23-30 are addressed to the student.

How you can help your students get the most out of this program:

1. Become familiar with the contents of the entire program before starting it.

2. Give students a copy of each story writing page in the program. The lesson pages can be photocopied beforehand and kept in individual student notebooks or pages can be photocopied as needed. If there is only one student, he or she may write in the book. However, to make this book non-consumable, the teacher should photocopy the following pages: 3-5, 7-10, 12, 15, 22-28, 30, 31, 37-43, 45, 46, 52-58, 60, 61, 66-72, 75-105. As students become more proficient at story writing, regular notebook paper can be substituted for the story writing forms.

3. Discuss each lesson thoroughly with the students.

4. Don't allow students to go on to new lessons before they have mastered current ones.

5. Read and check the rough draft of a student's story before allowing the student to write the final draft.

6. Make wall charts of the Editing Chart and the Parts of a Story Charts found in the Appendices. Constantly remind students to refer to these wall charts and to the Special Words Lists found in the Appendices.

7. Work on WIN lessons a minimum of three days per week.

8. Give students same-day feedback on their writing.

9. Use the material in the Appendices along with the regular WIN lessons. The material in the Appendices is designed to supplement, extend, and enhance the students' writing experiences in the rest of the program.

10. Use the Story Expansion section in Appendix A to evaluate student writing progress.

11. Do a quick review/discussion whenever you check a student-written story part, making "short note" suggestions on the student's story paper. These suggestions may be as simple as circling specific story elements in the left-hand margin which were either omitted or written in an unsatisfactory manner.

12. Provide each student with a folder or three-ring binder for filing his or her writing papers.

13. In addition to the **Introduction**, an excellent and an important component of the "WIN" program which should be read as soon as possible is the Story Expansion section found in Appendix A. This section provides the teacher with an expanding story model by which the teacher can evaluate the students' writing progress.

14. Lessons involving the use of direct quotations are in Appendix D. The authors recommend that teachers introduce the use of quotation marks no later than the third grade for most students. Even younger students can sometimes correctly use quotation marks. Direct quotations enliven a story and bring a "you-are-there" quality to it.

TO THE STUDENT:

Through this book you will enter the exciting world of story writing. Even if you don't think you are a good writer and don't like to write, you will find out just how easy it is to write an interesting story. When you have finished this book you will be writing stories you can be proud of and that other people will want to read.

Lessons 1 through 22 will sometimes have instructions for your teacher and sometimes instructions for you. Instructions meant especially for you will say "TO THE STUDENT." Lessons 23 through 30 have instructions written only to you.

How You Can Get the Most Out of This Program:

1. Read and follow the instructions meant especially for you **very carefully.**

2. Try to use your best handwriting.

3. Use a lot of imagination.

4. Keep all of your work in a folder or notebook so you can see how much better your stories are getting.

5. Think of story writing as a fun way to communicate with others.

WIN LEVEL II   LESSON 1

LESSON 1
THE FOUR PARAGRAPHS OF A STORY

Objective: To familiarize students with the four paragraphs of a story.

In order to help students learn how to write exciting and logical stories, this program teaches four major story sections. Each story section is presented in a separate paragraph:

First Section:	Setting Paragraph
Second Section:	Story Problem Paragraph
Third Section:	Action-Solution Paragraph
Fourth Section:	Conclusion Paragraph

During this lesson, the teacher will need to introduce the use of margin lines and indenting. The teacher should explain that the indentation of the first sentence of a paragraph tells the reader that a new idea has begun, that a change in what is being written about has happened. For these purposes, the teacher can use any of the model stories on pages 7, 8, 9, or 10. The teacher can have students locate the left margin line and indentations, and discuss the different ideas of each para- graph. The same, of course, could be done using a photocopied page from any basal text or novel. Having the students put P[1], P[2], P[3], and so on at the beginning of successive paragraphs can be instructive if using the photocopied page technique. It is quite important to emphasize that when writing stories all lines other than indented lines must hug the left margin line.

1

WIN LEVEL II   LESSON 1

Have the students turn to pages 3 and 4. On page 3 are the names of the four major story paragraphs and blank boxes. On page 4 discuss the parts which make up each of the four major story paragraphs.

TEACHING TIPS:
If there is only one student, he or she may write in the assignment pages in this book. However, to make this book nonconsumable, the teacher should photocopy pages 3, 4, and 5 for student use.

Pages 1 and 2:   Share the information with students.

Page 3:   Tell students the names of the four major paragraphs.

Page 4:   Tell students the names of sub-parts of each major paragraph.

Page 5:   Have students fill out this page.

WIN LEVEL II   LESSON 1

Title

**Setting
Paragraph** ———▶

**Story Problem
Paragraph** ———▶

**Action-Solution
Paragraph** ———▶

**Conclusion
Paragraph** ———▶

WIN LEVEL II   LESSON 1

Name

Title

**Setting
Paragraph** ⟶
Tells: When, Who,
Where, What,
Feelings and about
Starting Event.

**Story Problem
Paragraph** ⟶
Tells exciting things
characters Did, Saw,
Heard, Felt and Said
during the Starting
Event. Tells Scary or
Worrisome or Funny
Things about the
Story Problem.

**Action-Solution
Paragraph** ⟶
Tells important
things characters
Did, Saw, Heard, Felt
and Said while
solving Story
Problem.

**Conclusion
Paragraph**
Tells ending details
about solution: What
Charact. Did Next;
What Charact.
Learned; Brings back
Good Feelings.

4

WIN LEVEL II   LESSON 1

Name_____

STORY PARAGRAPHS

Write the names of the four major story paragraphs, in the correct sequence, on the lines below.

I. _____

II. _____

III. _____

IV. _____

WIN LEVEL II   LESSON 2

LESSON 2
PARTS OF THE PARAGRAPH

Objective: To familiarize students with the parts in each major paragraph.

The teacher will read the four stories on the next four pages and discuss the parts in each paragraph. The parts to be discussed are listed in the margin of each story.

TEACHING TIPS:
Page 7:   Ask student to read the story aloud and then to orally identify the specific sub-part (found in the margin) which describes each sentence in each paragraph. Some sentences, especially in the Story Problem Paragraph and the Action-Solution Paragraph, may have more than one sub-part which can correctly describe them.

Pages 8, 9, and 10:   Ask students to identify (using an outline format) the specific sub-part which describes each sentence in each paragraph.   **KEEP ANSWERS SHORT! Example of Outline Format for Page 8:**

  I.   **Setting**
        A.   **When**--morning
        B.   **Who**--Ricky, I
        C.   **Where**--hill
        D.   **What** (else is happening?) (detail sentences)--Our
              sleds were...
        E.   **Feelings**--excited (or anxious or impatient) (as
              implied by the words "ready to race")
        F.   **Starting Event**--We were ready to... (Usually the last
              sentence in the Setting.)
  II.   **Problem** (Sequence of sub-parts may vary. More than one
        sentence may be described by the same sub-part)
        A.   **Did**--Zoom! We were... I was going... But all of a
              sudden... I slowed... I almost...
        B.   **Saw**--I was out... Ricky was pretty... Ricky raced...
        C.   **Heard**--(Any sentence suggesting noise or sound.)
        D.   **Felt**--(Any sentence which states or implies feeling.)
        E.   **Said**--(or thought) I knew...
        F.   **Story Problem**--He was winning... (Usually the last
              sentence in the Story Problem Paragraph.)

Repeat the outlining process for the remaining two paragraphs.

6

WIN LEVEL II   LESSON 2

Title	**THE BALLOON RIDE**
Setting Paragraph Tells: When, Who, Where, What, Feelings and about Starting Event.	One summer afternoon my mom and I got out of the car in a large field. We looked at the hot-air balloons across the field and headed toward them. I was really excited. We were going on a hot-air balloon ride.
Story Problem Paragraph Tells exciting things characters Did, Saw, Heard, Felt and Said during the Starting Event. Tells Scary or Worrisome or Funny Things about the Story Problem.	We got in the basket under the balloon. The pilot took us high in the air. It was fun. Suddenly, a strong wind blew us right at a steep, rocky cliff. I was scared. We were going to crash!
Action-Solution Paragraph Tells important things characters Did, Saw, Heard, Felt and Said while solving Story Problem.	The pilot turned on the flame. Slowly, the balloon started to climb, but not fast enough. The steep cliff got closer and closer. Sharp rocks were everywhere. I tried not to cry. My mom hugged me close to her. Then, at the last minute, another wind lifted the balloon just over the edge of the cliff and saved us.
Conclusion Paragraph Tells ending details about solution: What Charact. Did Next; What Charact. Learned; Brings back Good Feelings.	Soon we landed safely in a field. We were glad to be back on the ground. I told my mom that I didn't want to go on a balloon ride again. I was happy to go home and so was my mom.

7

WIN LEVEL II   LESSON 2

Title   **THE GREAT RACE**

Setting
Paragraph ⟶
Tells: When, Who,
Where, What,
Feelings and about
Starting Event.

> The morning was snowy. Ricky and I stood at
> the top of the hill. Our sleds were right in front of us.
> We were ready to race to the bottom.

Story Problem
Paragraph ⟶
Tells exciting things
characters Did, Saw,
Heard, Felt and Said
during the Starting
Event. Tells Scary or
Worrisome or Funny
Things about the
Story Problem.

> Zoom! We were off! I was out in front. I was
> going fast. I knew I could win. Ricky was pretty far
> behind. But all of a sudden, my sled hit something. I
> slowed down. I almost tipped over. Ricky raced ahead
> of me. He was winning now.

Action-Solution
Paragraph ⟶
Tells important
things characters
Did, Saw, Heard, Felt
and Said while
solving Story
Problem.

> I straightened my sled. I pushed off hard with my
> leg, real hard. I was going faster and faster. He was
> half-way down already. There was only one way to
> catch up. I pushed back against the snow with my
> hands and arms. I did it again and again. I was
> catching up. Ricky turned around to see where I was.
> We were almost at the finish line. Ricky pushed hard
> with his hands. So did I. We crossed the finish line at
> the same time!

Conclusion
Paragraph
Tells ending details
about solution: What
Charact. Did Next;
What Charact.
Learned; Brings back
Good Feelings.

> Our sleds came to a stop. Ricky said that we tied.
> I told him he was lucky. I would have won if I hadn't
> tipped over. Next time, I would check for rocks under
> the snow first. It was a great race.

8

WIN LEVEL II   LESSON 2

Title	THE TREEHOUSE
Setting Paragraph → **Tells:** When, Who, Where, What, Feelings and about Starting Event.	One Saturday morning, Jenny and her brother Scott ran into their backyard. They had their hammers and nails. They raced to the tall tree. They couldn't wait to build their treehouse.
Story Problem Paragraph → **Tells** exciting things characters Did, Saw, Heard, Felt and Said during the Starting Event. Tells Scary or Worrisome or Funny Things about the Story Problem.	The wood was piled up next to the tree. The ladder leaned against it. Jenny climbed the ladder. Scott handed her some boards and climbed up, too. They pounded the boards into the big branches. The floor was done! They both stood happily on the floor they had built. Then a strange smell caught Jenny's attention. She turned around. It was a skunk! The skunk was spraying the floor of their treehouse. It was stinking up everything!
Action-Solution Paragraph → **Tells** important things characters Did, Saw, Heard, Felt and Said while solving Story Problem.	Jenny raced down the ladder. Scott swung down from the big branch. He got the garden hose. Jenny turned the water on fast. Scott climbed up the ladder and shot water on the skunk. It ran across the branch and jumped onto the garage roof. In a second, it was gone.
Conclusion Paragraph → **Tells** ending details about solution: What Charact. Did Next; What Charact. Learned; Brings back Good Feelings.	Jenny climbed up the ladder next to Scott. She held her nose shut and started spraying the floor of the treehouse. She told Scott that next time they should bring up the hose with them before they start hammering. Then she started spraying Scott. She told him that he stunk, too.

WIN LEVEL II   LESSON 2

Title   **THE LATE NIGHT FIRE**

Setting
Paragraph ——————▶   It was very late at night. My parents were gone. I
Tells: When, Who,   was home alone. I decided to make some cocoa and a
Where, What,
Feelings and about   sandwich and watch some TV. Then I heard a strange
Starting Event.   noise.

Story Problem
Paragraph ——————▶   I went to the front door to look around. Where
Tells exciting things   was the noise coming from? It was getting louder.
characters Did, Saw,
Heard, Felt and Said   Suddenly, I saw smoke coming up behind the barn.
during the Starting   The sound of fire roared in my ears. I rushed back
Event. Tells Scary or
Worrisome or Funny   into the house and called the fire department. When
Things about the   I looked outside again, the crackling fire was nearing
Story Problem.
                               the barn.

Action-Solution
Paragraph ——————▶   I raced to the shed and grabbed a hose.
Tells important   Nervously, I turned on the water. The fire still crept
things characters
Did, Saw, Heard, Felt   closer to the barn. Then the sounds of sirens could
and Said while   be heard as two big fire trucks came roaring up our
solving Story
Problem.   road. Soon firemen were spraying tons of water
                               around the barn and on the fire. The firemen were
                               winning the battle. They put out the fire and saved
                               our barn.

Conclusion
Paragraph
Tells ending details   While the firemen were putting away their hoses,
about solution: What   my parents came home. My mom and dad said that
Charact. Did Next;
What Charact.   I was a hero. I felt proud and thankful that the barn
Learned; Brings back   was saved. I learned how important firemen can be.
Good Feelings.

10

WIN LEVEL II   LESSON 3

LESSON 3
CONNECTING SENTENCES

Objective: To familiarize students with the function of connecting
            sentences.

TEACHING TIPS:
Pages 11, 12, 13 and 14:   Follow directions **PLUS** carefully point out to students
      how the **Starting Event Sentence** guides the students in "what to say" in the
      Story Problem Paragraph;
      how the **Story Problem Sentence** guides the students in "what to say" in the
      Action Solution Paragraph;
      how the **Solution Sentence** guides the students in "what to say" in the
      Conclusion Paragraph and how it leads to the **What was Learned Sentence.**

Page 15:   Follow directions. This page may be photocopied for student use.

TO THE STUDENT:

In order to make a story "flow" smoothly and to be easily
understood, this program has special connecting sentences which
connect the four major story paragraphs. These "connecting" sentences
are in bold print in the story "The Balloon Ride," so that students can
find them more easily.

Now read "The Balloon Ride" on the next page and pay special
attention to the bold print sentences. After you finish reading this story,
then read the pages called "How Connecting Sentences Work" which
follow the story.

WIN LEVEL II   **LESSON 3**

Title	**THE BALLOON RIDE**
Setting Paragraph ——▶ **Tells:** When, Who, Where, What, Feelings and about Starting Event.	One summer afternoon my mom and I got out of the car in a large field. We looked at the hot-air balloons across the field and headed toward them. I was really excited. **We were going on a hot-air balloon ride.**
Story Problem Paragraph ——▶ **Tells** exciting things characters Did, Saw, Heard, Felt and Said during the Starting Event. Tells Scary or Worrisome or Funny Things about the Story Problem.	We got in the basket under the balloon. The pilot took us high in the air. It was fun. Suddenly, a strong wind blew us right at a steep, rocky cliff. I was scared. **We were going to crash!**
Action-Solution Paragraph ——▶ **Tells** important things characters Did, Saw, Heard, Felt and Said while solving Story Problem.	The pilot turned on the flame. Slowly, the balloon started to climb, but not fast enough. The steep cliff got closer and closer. Sharp rocks were everywhere. I tried not to cry. My mom hugged me close to her. **Then, at the last minute, another wind lifted the balloon just over the edge of the cliff and saved us.**
Conclusion Paragraph ▶ **Tells** ending details about solution: What Charact. Did Next; What Charact. Learned; Brings back Good Feelings.	Soon we landed safely in a field. We were glad to be back on the ground. **I told my mom that I didn't want to ever go on a balloon ride again.** I was happy to go home and so was my mom.

12

WIN LEVEL II   LESSON 3

HOW CONNECTING SENTENCES WORK

Teacher Discussion: There are four connecting sentences in a story. These connecting sentences are explained below.

1. **Starting Event Sentence.** (In Setting Paragraph)
    a. **The Starting Event Sentence** tells or hints about something interesting or exciting the characters are starting to do **or** about something which is starting to happen to them.
    b. **The Starting Event Sentence** causes (or leads) characters to do certain things in the Story Problem Paragraph—this sentence connects the Setting Paragraph **to** the Story Problem Paragraph.
    c. **The Starting Event Sentence** is usually the last sentence in the Setting Paragraph.

2. **Story Problem Sentence.** (In Story Problem Paragraph)
    a. **The Story Problem Sentence** tells what Problem happens to the characters and hints that interesting and exciting events are going to happen (while solving the Problem) in the Action-Solution Paragraph.
    b. **The Story Problem Sentence** causes (or leads) characters to do certain things **or** causes certain things to happen to the characters in the Action-Solution Paragraph—this sentence connects the Story Problem Paragraph to the Action-Solution Paragraph.
    c. **The Story Problem Sentence** is usually the last sentence in the Story Problem Paragraph.

13

WIN LEVEL II   LESSON 3

HOW CONNECTING SENTENCES WORK

3. **Solution Sentence.** (In Action-Solution Paragraph)

   a. **The Solution Sentence** shows that the Story Problem has been solved.

   b. **The Solution Sentence** leads characters to think, **in the Conclusion Paragraph**, about the problem(s) they had—this sentence connects the Action-Solution Paragraph to the Conclusion Paragraph.

   c. **The Solution Sentence** is usually the last sentence in the Action-Solution Paragraph.

4. **What Was Learned Sentence.** (In Conclusion Paragraph)

   a. **The What-Was-Learned Sentence** shows what characters learned by telling how they would do things differently next time.

   b. **The What-Was-Learned Sentence** leads characters to express good feelings.

   c. **The What-Was-Learned Sentence** causes characters to think back about the other three connecting sentences and think, "How could I not have this problem again?".

   d. **The What-Was-Learned Sentence** is usually near the end of the Conclusion Paragraph.

14

WIN LEVEL II   LESSON 3

Name_____
THE FOUR CONNECTING SENTENCES
SUMMARY

Below, write the 4 sentences that connect the main ideas of the
story, "The Balloon Ride," together:

I. **Setting Paragraph**

The Starting Event Sentence: _____

_____

_____

II. **Story Problem Paragraph**

The Story Problem Sentence: _____

_____

_____

III. **Action-Solution Paragraph**

The Solution Sentence:_____

_____

_____

IV. **Conclusion Paragraph**

The What-Was-Learned Sentence: _____

_____

_____

_____

Now read the sentences in order as if they were the whole story.
They do tell the main ideas, but they miss the details!

15

WIN LEVEL II   LESSON 4

LESSON 4
INTRODUCTION OF SETTING PARAGRAPH PARTS

Objective: To reinforce students' understanding of Setting
Paragraph Parts.

Teacher discusses examples of Setting Paragraph Parts (When,
Who, Where, What, Feelings, and Starting Event Sentence) shown below.

I.   Setting Paragraph - tells. . .

   A.   **When** - the time the story is happening.

   Examples

   1. Early one morning. . .
   2. Late one afternoon. . .
   3. A long time ago. . .
   4. Just after breakfast. . .
   5. One warm summer day. . .
   6. One rainy night. . .
   7. Just after the sun came up. . .
   8. One Sunday morning. . .
   9. Sunset was almost at hand. . .
   10. Christmas Night had arrived. . .

   B.   **Who** - tells about the characters in the story.

   Examples

   1. Sally and Debbie
   2. My puppy and I
   3. John and his dog
   4. Mom and I
   5. My friend and I
   6. The little girl and her grandmother
   7. My mother and father

16

WIN LEVEL II   LESSON 4

INTRODUCTION OF SETTING PARAGRAPH PARTS

C.   **Where** - the place in which the story is happening.
      Examples
      1. At home
      2. In the backyard
      3. At the clubhouse
      4. Near the pond
      5. At the beach
      6. In the park
      7. On the porch
      8. At the game
      9. In a cave
      10. On a snowy mountain
      11. In the forest
      12. In the country

WIN LEVEL II   LESSON 4

INTRODUCTION OF SETTING PARAGRAPH PARTS

D.   **WHAT** - details about what else is happening which lead to the
      Starting Event.

Read the two sample Setting Paragraphs below. The words in
bold print in each Sample Setting are examples of the "What"
part in a Setting Paragraph.

#1 Sample Setting

It was a summer afternoon. **My mom and I got
out of the car** in a large field. **We looked at the
hot-air balloons across the field and headed
toward them.** I was really excited. We were
going on a hot-air balloon ride.

#2 Sample Setting

One Saturday morning, Jenny and her
brother Scott ran into their backyard. **They
had hammers and nails. They raced to the tall
tree.** They couldn't wait to build their
clubhouse.

18

WIN LEVEL II   LESSON 4

INTRODUCTION OF SETTING PARAGRAPH PARTS

E.   **Feelings** - tells or hints how the characters feel in
                    the beginning of the story.

Examples

1. I was really excited.

2. They couldn't wait to do it.

3. The day was going to be a great one!

4. We raced . . . for the beach!

                    . . . to the top of the hill!

                    . . . to the starting line!

5. My friend said, "Let's get going!"

F.   **Starting Event Sentence** - tells or hints about something
                    interesting or exciting the
                    characters are starting to do **or**
                    about something which is starting
                    to happen to them.

Examples

1. We were going on a balloon ride.

2. They couldn't wait to build their clubhouse.

3. Jenny and I were going canoeing.

4. My parents and I drove up into the snow.

5. Jeff and his sister opened the door to the
    haunted house.

6. Betty and Ann began climbing towards the old
    cave.

7. As we climbed the steep path, snow began to fall.

8. Ryan and Mark began building a snowman.

9. The big game would soon begin.

19

WIN LEVEL II   LESSON 5

LESSON 5
DISCUSSION OF SETTING PARAGRAPH PARTS

Teacher uses **The Balloon Ride** story on the next page as a model for giving examples of the parts of a **Setting Paragraph**. Students may follow along on their copy of page 7.

"The Balloon Ride" Setting Paragraph Discussion:

I.   **Setting Paragraph**

      A.   **When:**   **a summer afternoon**

      B.   **Who:**   **Mom and I**

      C.   **Where:**   **a large field**

      D.   **What:**   **My mom and I got out of the car.**
                                    We looked at the hot-air balloons and headed toward them.

      E.   **Feelings:** **really excited**

      F.   **Starting Event: We were going on a balloon ride.**

20

WIN LEVEL II   LESSON 5

Title _____   **THE BALLOON RIDE**

**Setting
Paragraph
Tells:** When, Who,
Where, What,
Feelings and about
Starting Event.

> One summer afternoon my mom and I got out of
> the car in a large field. We looked at the hot-air
> balloons across the field and headed toward them.
> I was really excited. We were going on a hot-air
> balloon ride.

**Story Problem
Paragraph
Tells** exciting things
characters Did, Saw,
Heard, Felt and Said
during the Starting
Event. Tells Scary or
Worrisome or Funny
Things about the
Story Problem.

> We got in the basket under the balloon. The
> pilot took us high in the air. It was fun. Suddenly, a
> strong wind blew right at a steep, rocky cliff. I was
> scared. We were going to crash!

**Action-Solution
Paragraph
Tells** important
things characters
Did, Saw, Heard,
Felt and Said
while solving
Story Problem.

> The pilot turned on the flame. Slowly, the balloon
> started to climb, but not fast enough. The steep cliff
> got closer and closer. Sharp rocks were everywhere.
> I tried not to cry. My mom hugged me close to her.
> Then, at the last minute, another wind lifted the
> balloon just over the edge of the cliff and saved us.

**Conclusion
Paragraph
Tells** ending details
about Solution:
What Charact. Did
Next; What
Charact. Learned;
Brings back Good
Feelings

> Soon we landed safely in a field. We were glad to
> be back on the ground. I told my mom that I didn't
> want to go on a balloon ride again. I was happy to
> go home and so was my mom.

WIN LEVEL II   LESSON 6

LESSON 6
IDENTIFYING PARTS OF THE SETTING PARAGRAPH

Objective: To provide students with opportunities to identify
Setting Paragraph Parts.

TEACHING TIP:
Pages 22, 23, 24, and 25 may be photocopied for student use.

TO THE STUDENT:

Step 1: Read the **Model Setting Paragraphs** on the next three pages.

Step 2: Find the words in each **Model Setting Paragraph** which are
examples of Setting Paragraph Parts (**When, Who, Where,
What, Feelings,** and **Starting Event**) shown at the bottom of
each page.

Step 3: Write the words you find in Step 2 next to the correct
Paragraph Parts at the bottom of each page.

Note: For instructional purposes, the parts of the **Setting Paragraph**
(and the other major paragraphs as well) are generally
presented in the same sequence in each lesson. However,
stories which you read or write may have a different sequence.

22

WIN LEVEL II   LESSON 6

Name ――――――――――――――――――――――――

Identify the parts of the Setting Paragraph below. Read the paragraph. Then on the lines below, tell or answer what each line asks about the paragraph. Some lines **may** not have an answer, but they usually will. Check carefully.

MODEL SETTING PARAGRAPH

The morning was snowy. Ricky and I stood at the top of the hill. Our sleds were right in front of us. We were ready to race to the bottom.

After reading the Setting Paragraph, tell . . .

1.   When the story happens: ――――――――――――――――

2.   Who the characters are: ――――――――――――――――

3.   Where story happens: ――――――――――――――――

4.   Feelings of characters: ――――――――――――――――

5.   What other things happen, leading to Starting Event:

       ――――――――――――――――――――――――――――

       ――――――――――――――――――――――――――――

6.   What other things happen, leading to Starting Event:

       ――――――――――――――――――――――――――――

       ――――――――――――――――――――――――――――

7.   Starting Event: ――――――――――――――――――――

       ――――――――――――――――――――――――――――

WIN LEVEL II   LESSON 6

Name _____

Identify the parts of the Setting Paragraph below. Read the paragraph. Then on the lines below, tell or answer what each line asks about the paragraph. Some lines **may** not have an answer, but they usually will. Check carefully.

MODEL SETTING PARAGRAPH

One Saturday morning, Jenny and her brother
Scott ran into their backyard. They had their hammers
and nails. They raced to the tall tree. They couldn't
wait to build their treehouse.

After reading the Setting Paragraph, tell . . .

1. When the story happens: _____

2. Who the characters are: _____

3. Where story happens: _____

4. Feelings of characters: _____

5. What other things happen, leading to Starting Event:

    _____

    _____

6. What other things happen, leading to Starting Event:

    _____

    _____

7. Starting Event: _____

    _____

24

WIN LEVEL II   LESSON 6

Name _____

Identify the parts of the Setting Paragraph below. Read the paragraph. Then on the lines below, tell or answer what each line asks about the paragraph. Some lines **may** not have an answer, but they usually will. Check carefully.

MODEL SETTING PARAGRAPH

Very late one night my parents were gone. I was
home alone. I decided to make some cocoa and a
sandwich and watch some TV. Then I heard a strange
noise.

After reading the Setting Paragraph, tell . . .

1.   When the story happens: _____

2.   Who the characters are: _____

3.   Where story happens: _____

4.   Feelings of characters: _____

5.   What other things happen, leading to Starting Event:

_____

_____

6.   What other things happen, leading to Starting Event:

_____

_____

7.   Starting Event: _____

_____

WIN LEVEL II   LESSON 7

LESSON 7
WRITING A PRACTICE SETTING PARAGRAPH

Objective: To provide students with guided practice in writing a
Setting Paragraph.

TEACHING TIPS:
Pages 26, 27, 28, and 29 may be photocopied for student use. You may use the
Pre-Story Writing Outline Forms (found in Appendix K) in place of the planning
form on page 27. Review the Story Editing Chart on page 29 with students.

TO THE STUDENT:

I.   Write a **Setting Paragraph** for a story about you and a little puppy.
     Remember to include the six key parts of a Setting:

     When (Ex. One day. . .Late one afternoon I. . .Last summer. . .Early one
     morning I. . .etc.)

     Who (Ex. a little puppy and I. . .)

     Where (Ex. at the park. . .near the school. . .etc.)

     What (Ex. playing soccer. . .mowing the lawn. . .eating a picnic lunch. .
     .etc.)

     Feelings (Ex. I was really excited. . . I dashed out the door. . . I didn't know
     what to do. . . etc.)

     Starting Event (Ex. We were ready for a day at the park. . . Then I heard
     my puppy barking loudly. . .)

II. Before you write your **Setting Paragraph,** complete the next page.
     You may use some of the ideas shown above to help you do this.

26

WIN LEVEL II   LESSON 7

Name_____

WRITING A PRACTICE SETTING PARAGRAPH

Complete this page. Use the information you write on this page to
help you write a **Setting Paragraph** on the next page.

I.   **Story Title:** _____

II. **Parts of the Setting Paragraph:**

   A.   **When** the story happened:_____

   B.   **Who** the story is about: _____

        _____

   C.   **Where** the story happened: _____

   D.   **What** else is happening: _____

        _____

   E.   **Feelings** of characters: _____

        _____

   F.   **Starting Event Sentence** (Tells or hints about something
        interesting or exciting the characters are starting to do
        or about something which is starting to happen to them):

        _____

        _____

        _____

III. After you write the **Setting Paragraph** on the next page, use the
      Story Editing chart on page 29 to make any needed changes.

IV.   Now begin writing your Setting Paragraph on the next page.

27

WIN LEVEL II   LESSON 7

PRACTICE SETTING PARAGRAPH   Name

Title

**Setting
Paragraph** ———▶
Tells: When, Who,
Where, What,
Feelings and about
Starting Event.

**Story Problem
Paragraph** ———▶
Tells exciting things
characters Did, Saw,
Heard, Felt and Said
during the Starting
Event. Tells Scary or
Worrisome or Funny
Things about the
Story Problem.

**Action-Solution
Paragraph** ———▶
Tells important
things characters
Did, Saw, Heard, Felt
and Said while
solving Story
Problem.

**Conclusion
Paragraph** ———▶
Tells ending details
about solution: What
Charact. Did Next;
What Charact.
Learned; Brings back   **(Save this page to use with page 43.)**
Good Feelings.   28

WIN LEVEL II   LESSON 7

STORY EDITING CHART

E D I T S Paper Carefully

E.   **Exciting Paragraphs.**

D.   **Details which describe.**

I.   **Indents Paragraphs.**

T.   **Title of Story.**

S.   **Spelling and Sentences and Sequence are correct.**

P.   **Punctuation is correct.**

C.   **Capitalization is correct.**

WIN LEVEL II   **LESSON 8**

Name_____

LESSON 8
DECISION TIME

Objective: To help students distinguish between exciting and
less exciting styles of writing.

Directions and Answer Sheet

Read the two Setting Paragraphs on the next page. Pay special
attention to the words used in each paragraph so that you are ready to
decide which of the two is written in a more exciting, interesting, or
powerful way. Be ready to tell why you think one paragraph is better
than the other. To do this, you must be able to tell **exactly which words**
make one paragraph better than the other. This is your evidence. Write
your answer in the box below with your evidence to support your opinion.

WIN LEVEL II   LESSON 8

DECISION TIME: Choosing Between Two Setting Paragraphs

Answer: Appendix B

#1

> Red, blue and yellow hot-air balloons rose up into
> the sunlit sky. I pulled my mom across the grassy field
> toward the balloons. The balloon ride was only minutes
> away.

#2

> Colorful hot-air balloons rose up into the sunlit
> sky. My mom and I went across the grassy field toward
> the balloons. The balloon ride was only minutes away.

WIN LEVEL II   LESSON 9

LESSON 9
INTRODUCTION OF STORY PROBLEM PARAGRAPH

Objective: To reinforce students' understanding of Story
Problem Paragraph Parts.

Teacher discusses examples of Story Problem Paragraph Parts
(Did, Saw, Heard, Felt, Said, and Story Problem) shown below.

I.   **Story Problem Paragraph** - tells exciting things

characters. . .

A.   **Did** because of Starting Event Sentence.

Examples

1.   We climbed on our surfboards.

2.   Carefully we started down the steep trail.

3.   The pilot started the engine.

4.   Betty and I skated over the frozen lake.

5.   Jeff and Mark looked through the window of the haunted
      house.

6.   Nervously we began to explore the cave.

B.   **Saw** because of the Starting Event Sentence.

Examples

1.   Overhead, the clouds got darker and darker.

2.   The fire began to spread through the trees.

3.   Waves ten feet tall came crashing down.

4.   Straight ahead were snow-covered mountains.

5.   We could see the lion pacing back and forth in his cage.

6.   Without warning, jets came diving towards us.

WIN LEVEL II   LESSON 9

INTRODUCTION OF STORY PROBLEM PARAGRAPH

C.   **Heard** because of the Starting Event Sentence.

Examples

1.   Loud thunder broke the silence.
2.   The sounds of sirens roared in our ears.
3.   The crowd cheered as the race began.
4.   A heavy rain pounded on the cabin roof.
5.   My kitten Socks purred softly while she slept.
6.   Streaks of lightning crackled overhead.

D.   **Felt** because of the Starting Event Sentence.

Examples

1.   My sister opened her present excitedly.
2.   I screamed as I began to fall.
3.   We were scared when the storm came.
4.   We could not wait for the game to begin.
5.   Our parents were proud of us for taking the leaves.
6.   I stopped and listened anxiously to the strange noise.

WIN LEVEL II   LESSON 9

INTRODUCTION OF STORY PROBLEM PARAGRAPH

E.   **Said** because of the Starting Event Sentence.

Examples

1.   I told my sister to be careful.

2.   We shouted for help when we became lost.

3.   My mother said that I was brave.

4.   The team cheered when I came up to bat.

5.   Ann whispered the secret to Judy.

6.   Mark asked, "Do you think it's safe?"
     Jeff answered, "I hope so."

F.   **Story Problem Sentence** - tells what problem happens to the characters and hints that interesting or exciting events are going to happen (while solving the Problem) in the Action-Solution Paragraph. It is usually the last sentence in the paragraph.

Examples

1.   The boat began to leak.

2.   Rocks began to fall and we were trapped in the cave.

3.   As the big race began, Mark fell and cut his knee.

4.   The city was going to tear down our clubhouse.

5.   Our team was losing the game.

6.   The kitten was trapped high in the tree.

34

WIN LEVEL II   LESSON 10

LESSON 10
DISCUSSION OF STORY PROBLEM PARAGRAPH

Objective: To provide students with a review of the function of
the Story Problem Paragraph Parts.

Teacher uses **The Balloon Ride** story on the next page as a model for
giving examples of the parts of a Story Problem Paragraph. Students
may follow along on their copy of page 7.

The Balloon Ride Story Problem Paragraph Discussion

II.   **Story Problem Paragraph Parts**

A.   **Did:**   We got in the basket . . .

                            The pilot took us high . . .

B.   **Saw:**   a steep rocky cliff . . .

C.   **Heard:**   a strong wind . . .

D.   **Felt:**   scared.

E.   **Story Problem:** We were going to crash.

35

WIN LEVEL II   LESSON 10

Title

THE BALLOON RIDE

Setting Paragraph ⟶
Tells: When, Who, Where, What, Feelings and about Starting Event.

> One summer afternoon my mom and I got out of the car in a large field. We looked at the hot-air balloons across the field and headed toward them. I was really excited. We were going on a hot-air balloon ride.

Story Problem Paragraph ⟶
Tells exciting things characters Did, Saw, Heard, Felt and Said during the Starting Event. Tells Scary or Worrisome or Funny Things about the Story Problem.

> We got in the basket under the balloon. The pilot took us high in the air. It was fun. Suddenly, a strong wind blew us right at a steep, rocky cliff. I was scared. We were going to crash!

Action-Solution Paragraph ⟶
Tells important things characters Did, Saw, Heard, Felt and Said while solving Story Problem.

> The pilot turned on the flame. Slowly, the balloon started to climb, but not fast enough. The steep cliff got closer and closer. Sharp rocks were everywhere. I tried not to cry. My mom hugged me close to her. Then, at the last minute, another wind lifted the balloon just over the edge of the cliff and saved us.

Conclusion Paragraph ⟶
Tells ending details about solution: What Charact. Did Next; What Charact. Learned; Brings back Good Feelings.

> Soon we landed safely in a field. We were glad to be back on the ground. I told my mom that I did not want to go on a balloon ride again. I was happy to go home and so was my mom.

WIN LEVEL II   LESSON 11

LESSON 11
IDENTIFYING PARTS OF THE STORY PROBLEM PARAGRAPH

Objective: To provide students with opportunities to identify
Story Problem Paragraph Parts.

TEACHING TIP:
Pages 37, 38, 39, and 40 may be photocopied for student use.

TO THE STUDENT:

Step 1:   Read the **Model Story Problem Paragraphs** on the next three
pages.

Step 2:   Find words in each **Model Story Problem Paragraph** which are
examples of Story Problem Paragraph Parts (**Did, Saw, Heard,
Felt, Said,** and **Story Problem**) shown at the bottom of each
page.

Step 3:   Write the words you find in Step 2 next to the correct
Paragraph Parts at the bottom of each page. **PLEASE NOTE:**
The **words** chosen from the sentences which occur **before the
bold vertical bar should be placed on the "During Starting
Event" lines**. **Words** chosen from the sentences which occur
**after the bold vertical bar should be placed on the "During
Story Problem" lines.**

37

WIN LEVEL II   LESSON 11

Name _____

Identify the parts of the Story Problem Paragraph below. Read the paragraph. Then on the lines below, tell or answer what each line asks about the paragraph. Some lines **may** not have an answer, but they usually will. Check carefully.

MODEL STORY PROBLEM PARAGRAPH

Zoom! We were off! I was out in front. I was going fast. I knew I could win. Ricky was pretty far behind. But all of a sudden, my sled hit something. I slowed down. I almost tipped over. Ricky raced ahead of me. He was winning now.

After reading the Story Problem Paragraph, tell what the characters . . .

	1. Did: _____
During	2. Saw: _____
Starting	3. Heard: _____
Event	4. Felt: _____
	5. Said: _____

- -

	1. Did: _____
During	2. Saw: _____
Story	3. Heard: _____
Problem	4. Felt: _____
	5. Tell Story Problem: _____

38

WIN LEVEL II   LESSON 11

Name_____

Identify the parts of the Story Problem Paragraph below. Read the paragraph. Then on the lines below, tell or answer what each line asks about the paragraph. Some lines **may** not have an answer, but they usually will. Check carefully.

MODEL STORY PROBLEM PARAGRAPH

| The wood was piled up next to the tree. The ladder |
| leaned against it. Jenny climbed the ladder. Scott hand- |
| ed her some boards and climbed up, too. They pounded |
| the boards into the big branches. The floor was done |
| They both stood happily on the floor they had built. |
| Then a strange smell caught Jenny's attention. She |
| turned around. It was a skunk! The skunk was spraying |
| the floor of their treehouse. It was stinking up everything. |

After reading the Story Problem Paragraph, tell what the characters . . .

During Starting Event
1. Did: _____
2. Saw: _____
3. Heard: _____
4. Felt: _____
5. Said: _____

- -

During Story Problem
1. Did: _____
2. Saw: _____
3. Heard: _____
4. Felt: _____
5. Tell Story Problem: _____

WIN LEVEL II   LESSON 11

Name_____

Identify the parts of the Story Problem Paragraph below. Read the paragraph. Then on the lines below, tell or answer what each line asks about the paragraph. Some lines **may** not have an answer, but they usually will. Check carefully.

MODEL STORY PROBLEM PARAGRAPH

I went to the front door to look around. Where was the noise coming from? It was getting louder. Suddenly, I saw smoke coming up behind the barn. The sound of fire roared in my ears. I rushed back into the house and called the fire department. When I looked outside again, the crackling fire was nearing the barn.

After reading the Story Problem Paragraph, tell what the characters . . .

During
Starting
Event
{
1. Did: _____
2. Saw: _____
3. Heard: _____
4. Felt: _____
5. Said: _____

- -

During
Story
Problem
{
1. Did: _____
2. Saw: _____
3. Heard: _____
4. Felt: _____
5. Tell Story Problem: _____

40

WIN LEVEL II   LESSON 12

LESSON 12
WRITING A PRACTICE STORY PROBLEM PARAGRAPH

Objective: To provide students with guided practice in writing a
Story Problem Paragraph.

TEACHING TIP:
Pages 41, 42, and 43 may be photocopied for student use. You may use the Pre-Story Writing Outline Forms (found in Appendix K) in place of the planning form on page 42.

TO THE STUDENT:

I.   Write a **Story Problem Paragraph** for a story about you and a little puppy. This paragraph should continue the story you began about a little puppy and you on page 28. Remember to include the six main parts of a **Story Problem Paragraph:**

Did (Example: The puppy ran by the swings . . . I began calling the puppy.)

Saw (Example: I watched as the puppy raced towards the pond.)

Heard (Example: Then I heard the barking of the puppy.)

Felt (Example: A frightened little girl. . .

Said (Example: . . . screamed, "Help! Help!")

Story Problem (Example: The little girl had fallen into the pond.)

II. Before you write your **Story Problem Paragraph**, complete the next page. You may use some of the ideas shown above to help you do this.

41

WIN LEVEL II   LESSON 12

Name _____

WRITING A PRACTICE STORY PROBLEM PARAGRAPH

Complete this page. Use the information you write on this page to
help you write a Story Problem Paragraph on the next page.

I. **Parts of the Story Problem Paragraph**

Exciting things characters:

A. **Did:** _____

_____

B. **Saw:** _____

_____

C. **Heard:** _____

_____

D. **Felt:** _____

_____

E. **Said:** _____

_____

F. **Story Problem:** _____

_____

II. After your write the **Story Problem Paragraph** on the next page, use
the Story Editing chart on page 44 to make any needed changes.

III. Now begin writing your **Story Problem Paragraph** on the next page.

42

WIN LEVEL II   LESSON 12

PRACTICE STORY PROBLEM PARAGRAPH
(Continued from page 28.)   Name _____

Title _____

Setting Paragraph ———▶ **Tells:** When, Who, Where, What, Feelings and about Starting Event.

Story Problem Paragraph ———▶ **Tells** exciting things characters Did, Saw, Heard, Felt and Said during the Starting Event. Tells Scary or Worrisome or Funny Things about the Story Problem.

Action-Solution Paragraph ———▶ **Tells** important things characters Did, Saw, Heard, Felt and Said while solving Story Problem.

Conclusion Paragraph ———▶ **Tells** ending details about solution: What Charact. Did Next; What Charact. Learned; Brings back Good Feelings.

(Save this page to use with page 58.)

43

WIN LEVEL II

LESSON 12

STORY EDITING CHART
E D I T S Paper Carefully

E.   **Exciting Paragraphs.**

D.   **Details which describe.**

I.   **Indents Paragraphs.**

T.   **Title of Story.**

S.   **Spelling and Sentences and Sequence are correct.**

P.   **Punctuation is correct.**

C.   **Capitalization is correct.**

WIN LEVEL II   LESSON 13

Name_____

LESSON 13
DECISION TIME

Objective: To help students distinguish between exciting and
less exciting styles of writing.

Directions and Answer Sheet

Read the two Story Problem Paragraphs on the next page. Pay
special attention to the words used in each paragraph so that you are
ready to decide which of the two is written in a more exciting, interesting,
or powerful way. Be ready to tell why you think one paragraph is better
than the other. To do this, you must be able to tell **exactly which words**
make one paragraph better than the other. This is your evidence. Write
your answer in the box below with your evidence to support your opinion.

45

WIN LEVEL II   LESSON 13

DECISION TIME: Choosing Between Two Story Problem Paragraphs

#1   Answer: Appendix B

> Suddenly, a strong wind blew us right at a steep, rocky cliff. The basket jerked back and forth. The pilot, my mom and I grabbed the side, but the basket jerked back the other way and we fell to the floor. The wind was howling past us. The pilot yelled at us to stay down. He pulled himself up. I knew we could crash at any time!

#2

> Suddenly, a strong wind blew us right at a steep, rocky cliff. The basket jerked back and forth. My mom and I fell to the floor. I was scared. I knew we could crash at any time!

WIN LEVEL II   LESSON 14

LESSON 14
INTRODUCTION OF ACTION-SOLUTION PARAGRAPH

Objective: To reinforce students' understanding of Action-
Solution Paragraph Parts.

Teacher discusses examples of Action-Solution Paragraph Parts
(Did, Saw, Heard, Felt, Said, and Solution of Story Problem) shown below.

I. **Action-Solution Paragraph** - tells important things characters . .

    A. **Did** while solving the Story Problem.

    Examples

      1. We swam towards the raft.

      2. Jeff hurried to the phone and called the police.

      3. The pilot turned the plane sharply at the last moment.

      4. We placed the ladder by the window of the smoke-filled
         room.

      5. My sister dropped me one end of the rope as I lay injured in
         the deep pit.

    B. **Saw** while solving the Story Problem.

    Examples

      1. Hungry sharks were circling our leaking boat.

      2. The tired runners were struggling towards the finish line.

      3. Steep canyon walls were all around us.

      4. The out-of-control sled gained speed as it headed down the
         mountain.

      5. We could see the tiny raft bobbing in the water.

WIN LEVEL II   LESSON 14

INTRODUCTION OF ACTION-SOLUTION PARAGRAPH

C.   **Heard** while solving the Story Problem.

Examples

1. The dog barked loudly at the stranger.

2. I could barely hear their shouts for help.

3. The night was strangely quiet.

4. Sally and Debbie listened to the roar of the storm.

5. Two policemen jumped out as the car screeched to a halt.

6. He was gasping for breath as he climbed the steep mountain.

D.   **Felt** while solving the Story Problem.

Examples

1. Ann screamed with excitement when she found her puppy.

2. Mark and Jeff became concerned when they heard a growl.

3. The crowd grew silent when the player was hurt.

4. My sister was sad when her best friend moved away.

5. We were scared that our team would lose.

6. Ricky raced to his house with his new trophy.

WIN LEVEL II   LESSON 14

INTRODUCTION OF ACTION-SOLUTION PARAGRAPH

E.   **Said** while solving the Story Problem.
      Examples
      1. I called my brother's name but he did not answer.
      2. Jeff asked Mark to go get some help.
      3. Feeling lost, Robin began to cry for her mother.
      4. Ricky wondered if they would get out of the cave safely.
      5. The guide said that the path was narrow.
      6. Ann told her brother to be brave.

F.   **Solution Sentence** - shows that the Story Problem
                              has been solved.
      Examples
      1. Rob and Mike moved the rock and escaped from the cave.
      2. I climbed the ladder and brought the kitten safely down
         from the tree.
      3. Jenny put her brother on a log and pushed him safely to
         shore.
      4. Andy hit a home run and won the game.
      5. A sudden wind pushed our boat across the finish line first.
      6. The brave dog pulled the little girl from the pond.

WIN LEVEL II   LESSON 15

LESSON 15
DISCUSSION OF ACTION-SOLUTION PARAGRAPH

Objective: To provide students with a review of the function of
the Action-Solution Paragraph Parts.

Teacher uses **The Balloon Ride** story on the next page as a model for
giving examples of the parts of an **Action-Solution Paragraph.** Students
may follow along on their copy of page 7.

The Balloon Ride Action-Solution Paragraph Discussion

III. **Action-Solution Paragraph Parts**

    A.   **Did:** The pilot turned on the flame . . .

    B.   **Saw:** balloon began to climb . . .

                steep cliff got closer and closer . . .

                sharp rocks everywhere.

    C.   **Felt:** tried not to cry . . .

    D.   **Did:** Mom hugged me close to her . . .

    E.   **Solution Sentence:** another wind lifted the balloon over the
edge of the cliff and saved us.

50

WIN LEVEL II   LESSON 15

Title	**THE BALLOON RIDE**
Setting Paragraph ⟶ **Tells:** When, Who, Where, What, Feelings and about Starting Event.	One summer afternoon my mom and I got out of the car in a large field. We looked at the hot-air balloons across the field and headed toward them. I was really excited. We were going on a hot-air balloon ride.
Story Problem Paragraph ⟶ **Tells** exciting things characters Did, Saw, Heard, Felt and Said during the Starting Event. Tells Scary or Worrisome or Funny Things about the Story Problem.	We got in the basket under the balloon. The pilot took us high in the air. It was fun. Suddenly, a strong wind blew us right at a steep, rocky cliff. I was scared. We were going to crash!
Action-Solution Paragraph ⟶ **Tells** important things characters Did, Saw, Heard, Felt and Said while solving Story Problem.	The pilot turned on the flame. Slowly, the balloon started to climb, but not fast enough. The steep cliff got closer and closer. Sharp rocks were everywhere. I tried not to cry. My mom hugged me close to her. Then, at the last minute, another wind lifted the balloon just over the edge of the cliff and saved us.
Conclusion Paragraph ⟶ **Tells** ending details about solution: What Charact. Did Next; What Charact. Learned; Brings back Good Feelings.	Soon we landed safely in a field. We were glad to be back on the ground. I told my mom that I did not want to go on a balloon ride again. I was happy to go home and so was my mom.

WIN LEVEL II   LESSON 16

LESSON 16
IDENTIFYING PARTS OF THE ACTION-SOLUTION PARAGRAPH

Objective: To provide students with opportunities to identify
Action-Solution Paragraph Parts.

TEACHING TIP:
Pages 52, 53, 54, and 55 may be photopcopied for student use.

TO THE STUDENT:

Step 1:   Read the **Model Action-Solution Paragraphs** on the next three
              pages.

Step 2:   Find words in each **Model Action-Solution Paragraph** which
              are examples of Action-Solution Paragraph Parts (**Did, Saw,
              Heard, Felt, Said** and **Solution**) shown at the bottom of each
              page.

Step 3:   Write the words you find in Step 2 next to the correct
              Paragraph Parts at the bottom of each page.

52

WIN LEVEL II   LESSON 16

Name _____

Identify the parts of the Action-Solution Paragraph below. Read the paragraph. Then on the lines below, tell or answer what each line asks about the paragraph. Some lines **may** not have an answer, but they usually will. Check carefully.

MODEL ACTION-SOLUTION PARAGRAPH

I straightened my sled. I pushed off hard with my
leg—real hard. I was going faster and faster. He was half-
way down already. There was only one way to catch up.
I pushed back against the snow with my hands and arms.
I did it again and again. I was catching up. Ricky turned
around to see where I was. We were almost at the finish
line. Ricky pushed hard with his hands; so did I. We
crossed the finish line at the same time!

After reading the Action-Solution Paragraph, tell what the characters . . .

1.   Did: _____

2.   Did: _____

3.   Saw: _____

4.   Saw: _____

5.   Heard: _____

6.   Felt: _____

7.   Said: _____

8.   Said: _____

Now tell . . .

9.   The Solving Sentence _____

WIN LEVEL II   LESSON 16

Name _____

    Identify the parts of the Action-Solution Paragraph below. Read the paragraph. Then on the lines below, tell or answer what each line asks about the paragraph. Some lines **may** not have an answer, but they usually will. Check carefully.

MODEL ACTION-SOLUTION PARAGRAPH

Jenny raced down the ladder. Scott swung down
from the big branch. He got the garden hose. Jenny
turned the water on fast. Scott climbed up the ladder and
shot water on the skunk. It ran across a branch and
jumped onto the garage roof. In a second, it was gone.

After reading the Action-Solution Paragraph, tell what the characters . . .

1.   Did:_____

2.   Did:_____

3.   Saw:_____

4.   Saw:_____

5.   Heard:_____

6.   Felt:_____

7.   Said:_____

8.   Said:_____

Now tell . . .

9.   The Solving Sentence_____

WIN LEVEL II   LESSON 16

Name _____

Identify the parts of the Action-Solution Paragraph below. Read the
paragraph. Then on the lines below, tell or answer what each line asks
about the paragraph. Some lines **may** not have an answer, but they
usually will. Check carefully.

MODEL ACTION-SOLUTION PARAGRAPH

I raced to the shed and grabbed a hose. Nervously,
I turned on the water. The fire still crept closer to the
barn. Then the sounds of sirens could be heard as two
big fire trucks came roaring up our road. Soon firemen
were spraying tons of water around the barn and on the
fire. The firemen were winning the battle. They put out
the fire and saved our barn.

After reading the Action-Solution Paragraph, tell what the characters . . .

1.   Did: _____

2.   Did: _____

3.   Saw: _____

4.   Saw: _____

5.   Heard: _____

6.   Felt: _____

7.   Said: _____

8.   Said: _____

Now tell . . .

9.   The Solving Sentence _____

55

WIN LEVEL II   LESSON 17

LESSON 17
WRITING A PRACTICE ACTION-SOLUTION PARAGRAPH

Objective: To provide students with guided practice in writing
an Action-Solution Paragraph.

TEACHING TIP:
Pages 56, 57, and 58 may be photocopied for student use. You may use the Pre-Story Writing Outline Forms in Appendix K in place of the planning form on page 57.

TO THE STUDENT:

I.   Write an **Action-Solution Paragraph** for a story about you and a little puppy. This paragraph should continue the story you wrote about "you and a little puppy" on pages 28 and 43.

Remember to include the six main parts of an **Action-Solution Paragraph:**

Did (Example: I dropped my sandwich and jumped to my feet.)

Saw (Example: a crowd of children running towards the pond.)

Heard (Example: For a moment I was so afraid I couldn't move.)

Said (Example: Someone yelled, "What can we do? What can we do?")

Solution (Example: I waded out to the little girl . . . Holding on to a low tree branch, I grabbed the little girl.)

II. Before you write your Action-Solution Paragraph complete the next page. You may use some of the ideas shown above to help you do this.

56

WIN LEVEL II   LESSON 17

Name——————————————————

WRITING A PRACTICE ACTION-SOLUTION PARAGRAPH

Complete this page. Use the information you write on this page to
help you write an Action-Solution Paragraph on the next page.

I.   **Parts of the Action-Solution Paragraph**
     Important things characters:
     A.   **Did:** _____

     B.   **Saw:** _____
          _____
     C.   **Heard:** _____
          _____
     D.   **Felt:** _____
          _____
     E.   **Said:** _____
          _____
     F.   **Conclusion:** _____
          _____

II. After you write the **Action-Solution Paragraph** on the next page, use
     the Story Editing Chart on page 59 to make any needed changes.

III. Now begin writing your **Action-Solution Paragraph** on the next
     page.

57

WIN LEVEL II   LESSON 17

PRACTICE ACTION-SOLUTION PARAGRAPH
(Continued from page 43.)

Name _____

Title _____

Setting Paragraph →
Tells: When, Who, Where, What, Feelings and about Starting Event.

Story Problem Paragraph →
Tells exciting things characters Did, Saw, Heard, Felt and Said during the Starting Event. Tells Scary or Worrisome or Funny Things about the Story Problem.

Action-Solution Paragraph →
Tells important things characters Did, Saw, Heard, Felt and Said while solving Story Problem.

Conclusion Paragraph →
Tells ending details about solution: What Charact. Did Next; What Charact. Learned; Brings back Good Feelings.

(Save this page to use with page 72.)

58

WIN LEVEL II   LESSON 17

STORY EDITING CHART
E D I T S Paper Carefully

E.   **Exciting Paragraphs**

D.   **Details which describe.**

I.   **Indents Paragraphs.**

T.   **Title of Story.**

S.   **Spelling and Sentences and Sequence are correct.**

P.   **Punctuation is correct.**

C.   **Capitalization is correct.**

WIN LEVEL II   LESSON 18

Name _____

LESSON 18
DECISION TIME

Objective: To help students distinguish between exciting and
less exciting styles of writing.

Directions and Answer Sheet

Read the two Action-Solution Paragraphs on the next page. Pay
special attention to the words used in each paragraph so that you are
ready to decide which of the two is written in a more exciting, interesting,
or powerful way. Be ready to tell why you think one paragraph is better
than the other. To do this, you must be able to tell **exactly which words**
make one paragraph better than the other. This is your evidence. Write
your answer in the box below with your evidence to support your opinion.

WIN LEVEL II   LESSON 18

Decision Time: Choosing Between Two Action-Solution Paragraphs
#1
                                              Answer: Appendix B

> The pilot pulled himself up and turned on the burner. Flames went up and into the balloon. The balloon began to climb, but not fast enough. I could see the pilot was still scared. I let go of my mom's hand and pulled myself up. The cliff was only ten feet away. Huge, sharp rocks were everywhere. Then, at the last minute, another wind lifted the balloon just over the edge of the cliff and saved us.

#2

> The pilot pulled himself up and turned on the burner. Roaring flames burst up and into the balloon. The balloon began to climb, but not fast enough. The pilot's face turned white with fear. I let go of my mom's hand and pulled myself up. The cliff was only ten feet away. Huge, sharp rocks were pointed at us. Then, at the last minute, another wind lifted the balloon just over the edge of the cliff and saved us.

61

WIN LEVEL II   LESSON 19

LESSON 19
INTRODUCTION OF CONCLUSION PARAGRAPH

Objective: To reinforce students' understanding of Conclusion
Paragraph Parts.

Teacher discusses examples of Conclusion Paragraph Parts
(Ending details about Solution, What characters did next, What
characters learned, and Brings back Good Feelings) shown below.

I. **Conclusion Paragraph** - (Ending Details About Solution tells . . .

A.   **What Characters Did Next**
      Examples
      1.   After rescuing the kitten, I put the ladder away.
      2.   When the storm stopped, Betty and her brother started
           for home.
      3.   Mark took off his skis at the end of the race.
      4.   Our team received a trophy for winning the game.
      5.   Andy hurried home to show his mother his prize.
      6.   After reach the shore, we put the leaky boat on a trailer.
      7.   Then we took the kitten into the house.
      8.   We hurried through the forest.
      9.   He brushed off the snow as he headed for the lodge.
      10. We attended an exciting ceremony.

62

WIN LEVEL II   LESSON 19

INTRODUCTION OF CONCLUSION PARAGRAPH

B. **What Character Learned**

Examples

1. We told our mom that we would watch the kitten more carefully.

2. Betty and her brother would bring their raincoats next time.

3. Mark decided he needed more skiing lessons.

4. We realized we would not have won the trophy without lots of practice.

5. Andy thought how special his mom was.

6. "Next time I'll check the boat for leaks," I said as I ate my pizza.

C. **Brings Back Good Feelings**

Examples

1. My sister and I were happy to have our kitten safely back.

2. They were thankful to reach home without being hurt by the storm.

3. He also felt excited about races in the future.

4. This had been one of the most exciting days in our lives.

5. Andy felt very proud when he showed his prize to his mother.

6. What a great day this had been—going boating and eating pizza too.

WIN LEVEL II   LESSON 20

LESSON 20
DISCUSSION OF CONCLUSION PARAGRAPH

Objective: To provide students with a review of the function of
the Conclusion Paragraph Parts.

Teacher uses **The Balloon Ride** story on the next page as a model for
giving examples of the parts of a **Conclusion Paragraph.** Students may
follow along on their copy of page 7.

"The Balloon Ride" Conclusion Paragraph Discussion

IV.   **Conclusion Paragraph Parts (Ending Details About
        Solution)**

   A.   **What Characters Did Next: We landed safely in a field. We
          were glad to be back on the ground.**

   B.   **What Characters Learned: I told my mom that I did not want
          to go on a balloon ride again.**

   C.   **Brings Back Good Feelings: I was happy to go home and so
          was my mom.**

64

WIN LEVEL II   LESSON 20

Title   **THE BALLOON RIDE**

**Setting
Paragraph** ————➤
Tells: When, Who,
Where, What,
Feelings and about
Starting Event.

> One summer afternoon my mom and I got out of
> the car in a large field. We looked at the hot-air
> balloons across the field and headed toward them.
> I was really excited. We were going on a hot-air
> balloon ride.

**Story Problem
Paragraph** ————➤
Tells exciting things
characters Did, Saw,
Heard, Felt and Said
during the Starting
Event. Tells Scary or
Worrisome or Funny
Things about the
Story Problem.

> We got in the basket under the balloon. The
> pilot took us high in the air. It was fun. Suddenly, a
> strong wind blew us right at a steep, rocky cliff. I was
> scared. We were going to crash!

**Action-Solution
Paragraph** ————➤
Tells important
things characters
Did, Saw, Heard, Felt
and Said while
solving Story
Problem.

> The pilot turned on the flame. Slowly, the balloon
> started to climb, but not fast enough. The steep cliff
> got closer and closer. Sharp rocks were everywhere.
> I tried not to cry. My mom hugged me close to her.
> Then, at the last minute, another wind lifted the
> balloon just over the edge of the cliff and saved us.

**Conclusion
Paragraph**
Tells ending details
about solution: What
Charact. Did Next;
What Charact.
Learned; Brings back
Good Feelings.

> Soon we landed safely in a field. We were glad to
> be back on the ground. I told my mom that I did not
> want to go on a balloon ride again. I was happy to
> go home and so was my mom.

65

WIN LEVEL II   LESSON 21

LESSON 21
IDENTIFYING PARTS OF THE CONCLUSION PARAGRAPH

Objective: To provide students with opportunities to identify Conclusion Paragraph Parts.

TEACHING TIP:
Pages 66, 67, 68, and 69 may be photocopied for student use.

TO THE STUDENT:

Step 1: Read the **Model Conclusion Paragraphs** on the next three pages.

Step 2: Find words in each **Model Conclusion Paragraph** which are examples of Conclusion Paragraph Parts (**Ending Details About Solution; What Characters Did Next; What Characters Learned,** and **Brings Back Good Feelings**) shown at the bottom of each page.

Step 3: Write the words you find in Step 2 next to the correct Paragraph Parts at the bottom of each page.

66

WIN LEVEL II   LESSON 21

Name_____

Identify the parts of the Conclusion Paragraph below. Read the
paragraph. Then on the lines below, tell or answer what each line asks
about the paragraph. Some lines **may** not have an answer, but they
usually will. Check carefully.

MODEL CONCLUSION PARAGRAPH

Our sleds came to a stop. Ricky said we tied. I told
him he was lucky. I would have won if I had not tipped
over. Next time, I would check for rocks under the snow
first. It was a great race.

After reading the Conclusion Paragraph, tell . . .

1.   What characters did next: _____

       _____

2.   What characters did next: _____

       _____

3.   What characters learned: _____

       _____

4.   Words that bring back Good Feelings: _____

       _____

67

WIN LEVEL II   LESSON 21

Name_____

Identify the parts of the Conclusion Paragraph below. Read the paragraph. Then on the lines below, tell or answer what each line asks about the paragraph. Some lines **may** not have an answer, but they usually will. Check carefully.

MODEL CONCLUSION PARAGRAPH

| Jenny climbed up the ladder next to Scott. She held |
| her nose shut and started spraying the floor of the |
| treehouse. She told Scott that next time they should |
| bring up the hose with them before they start |
| hammering. Then she started spraying Scott. She told |
| him that he stunk, too. |
| |
| |

After reading the Conclusion Paragraph, tell . . .

1. What characters did next:_____

_____

2. What characters did next:_____

_____

3. What characters learned: _____

_____

4. Words that bring back Good Feelings: _____

_____

68

WIN LEVEL II   LESSON 21

Name_____

Identify the parts of the Conclusion Paragraph below. Read the
paragraph. Then on the lines below, tell or answer what each line asks
about the paragraph. Some lines **may** not have an answer, but they
usually will. Check carefully.

MODEL CONCLUSION PARAGRAPH

While the firemen were putting away their hoses,
my parents came home. My mom and dad said that I
was a hero. I felt proud. I was thankful the barn was
saved. I learned how important firemen can be.

After reading the Conclusion Paragraph, tell . . .

1.   What characters did next:_____

      _____

2.   What characters did next:_____

      _____

3.   What characters learned: _____

      _____

4.   Words that bring back Good Feelings: _____

      _____

69

WIN LEVEL II   LESSON 22

LESSON 22
WRITING A PRACTICE CONCLUSION PARAGRAPH

Objective: To provide students with guided practice in writing a
Conclusion Paragraph.

TEACHING TIP:
Pages 70, 71, and 72 may be photocopied for student use. You may use the Pre-
Story Writing Outline Forms in Appendix K in place of the planning form on page
71.

TO THE STUDENT:

I.   Write a **Conclusion Paragraph** for a story about "you and a little

     puppy." This paragraph should continue the story you wrote on

     pages 28, 43, and 58.

     REMEMBER TO INCLUDE the three main parts of a **Conclusion**

     Paragraph:

     What Character Did Next: (Example: I sat down to rest after saving

     the little girl.

     What the Characters Learned: (Example: I know now parks can be

     fun, but ponds can be dangerous.)

     Brings Back Good Feelings: (Example: I was glad the little girl was

     safe, and I felt proud of my puppy.)

II. Before you write your Conclusion Paragraph, complete the next

     page. You may use some of the ideas shown above to help you do

     this.

70

WIN LEVEL II   LESSON 22

Name_____

WRITING A PRACTICE CONCLUSION PARAGRAPH

Complete this page. Use the information you write on this page to help you write a Conclusion Paragraph on the next page.

I. **Parts of the Conclusion Paragraph**
   A. **What Character Did Next:** _____
   _____
   _____

   B. **What the Characters Learned:** _____
   _____
   _____

   C. **Brings Back Good Feelings:** _____
   _____
   _____

II. After you write the Conclusion Paragraph on the next page, use the Story Editing Chart on page 73 to make any needed changes.

III. Now begin writing your Conclusion Paragraph on the next page.

71

WIN LEVEL II   LESSON 22

PRACTICE CONCLUSION PARAGRAPH
(Continued from page 58.)   Name _____
Title _____

**Setting
Paragraph** ———▶
Tells: When, Who,
Where, What,
Feelings and about
Starting Event.

**Story Problem
Paragraph** ———▶
Tells exciting things
characters Did, Saw,
Heard, Felt and Said
during the Starting
Event. Tells Scary or
Worrisome or Funny
Things about the
Story Problem.

**Action-Solution
Paragraph** ———▶
Tells important
things characters
Did, Saw, Heard, Felt
and Said while
solving Story
Problem.

**Conclusion
Paragraph** ———▶
Tells ending details
about solution: What
Charact. Did Next;
What Charact.
Learned; Brings back
Good Feelings.

72

WIN LEVEL II   LESSON 22

STORY EDITING CHART
E D I T S Paper Carefully

E.   **Exciting Paragraphs.**

D.   **Details which describe.**

I.   **Indents Paragraphs.**

T.   **Title of Story.**

S.   **Spelling and Sentences and Sequence are correct.**

P.   **Punctuation is correct.**

C.   **Capitalization is correct.**

WIN LEVEL II   LESSON 22

IMPORTANT NOTE TO THE TEACHER:

Lessons 23 through 30 of the WIN Level II book are primarily addressed to the student.

However, individual children will vary in the amount of help and guidance needed, so the teacher should be available to discuss and review the story writing process and to give direction and suggestions. Students should be encouraged to refer to the wall charts on Editing and Parts of a Story and to the Special Words Lists found in the Appendices.

If there is only one student, he or she may write in the spaces provided in the book. To make this book nonconsumable, the student may either write on notebook paper or the teacher may photocopy pages 75-105 for student use.

WIN LEVEL II   LESSON 23

Name_____

LESSON 23
DECISION TIME

Objective: To help students distinguish between exciting and less
exciting styles of writing.

Directions and Answer Sheet

Read the two Conclusion Paragraphs on the next page. Pay special
attention to the words used in each paragraph so that you are ready to
decide which of the two is written in a more exciting, interesting, or
powerful way. Be ready to tell why you think one paragraph is better
than the other. To do this, you must be able to tell **exactly which words**
make one paragraph better than the other. This is your evidence. Write
your answer in the box below with your evidence to support your opinion.

WIN LEVEL II   LESSON 23

DECISION TIME: Choosing Between Two Conclusion Paragraphs

Answer: Appendix B

#1

> Before long, we landed safely in a field. We were
> glad to be back on the ground. When we sat down on the
> grass, I told my mom that from now on I'd rather ride
> on things that stay on the ground. She laughed and
> said that she agreed.

#2

> Before long, the thump of our basket hitting the
> ground seemed like the most wonderful sound I'd ever
> heard. My feet crunching the grass as I stepped out
> of the basket was the next best sound. When we
> sat down on the grass, I told my mom that from now on
> I'd rather ride on things that stay on the ground. She
> laughed and said that she agreed.

76

WIN LEVEL II   LESSON 24

LESSON 24
WRITING A SETTING PARAGRAPH

Objective: To give students independent practice in writing a Setting Paragraph.

TO THE STUDENT:

Write a Setting Paragraph on the Four-boxed Story Form on page 79. Before you begin writing this paragraph, your teacher will review the parts of the Setting with you.

When you are ready to begin writing your Setting Paragraph, your teacher may suggest several ideas for the Setting, or, instead, your teacher may choose to have you write about a rafting trip. Shown just below is a Starting Event Sentence about a rafting trip:

"We pushed the raft into the water and began our river adventure."

To help you organize your ideas for the Setting Paragraph, before you begin writing the paragraph on the Four-boxed Story Form on page 79, write some ideas on the Clustering form on the next page. ("Clustering" in the WIN Program means writing down key words which relate to an important thought or idea.) Then, write the Setting Paragraph. After you write your paragraph, use the Story Editing Chart on page H-1 in the Appendix to make any needed changes on page 79.

WIN LEVEL II   LESSON 24

CLUSTERING SHEET   NAME_____

TITLE _____

SETTING PARAGRAPH

WHEN

WHO

WHERE

WHAT

FEELINGS

STARTING EVENT

STORY PROBLEM PARAGRAPH

Did-Saw-Heard-Felt-Said-Problem

ACTION-SOLUTION PARAGRAPH

Did-Saw-Heard-Felt-Said-Solution

CONCLUSION PARAGRAPH

Did Next-Learned-Feel

WIN LEVEL II   LESSON 24

WRITING A SETTING PARAGRAPH   Name

Title

Setting Paragraph ⟶
Tells: When, Who, Where, What, Feelings and about Starting Event.

Story Problem Paragraph ⟶
Tells exciting things characters Did, Saw, Heard, Felt and Said during the Starting Event. Tells Scary or Worrisome or Funny Things about the Story Problem.

Action-Solution Paragraph ⟶
Tells important things characters Did, Saw, Heard, Felt and Said while solving Story Problem.

Conclusion Paragraph
Tells ending details about solution: What Charact. Did Next; What Charact. Learned; Brings back Good Feelings.

(Save this page for use with page 82.)

79

WIN LEVEL II   **LESSON 25**   LESSON 25

WRITING A STORY PROBLEM PARAGRAPH

Objective: To give students independent practice in writing a Story
Problem Paragraph.

TO THE STUDENT:

Write a Story Problem Paragraph on the Four-boxed Story Form on
page 82, continuing the story that you began on page 79. Before you
begin writing this paragraph, your teacher will review the parts of the
Story Problem Paragraph with you.

To help you organize your ideas for writing the Story Problem
Paragraph, before you begin writing the paragraph on page 82, write
some ideas on the Clustering form on the next page. Then, write your
Story Problem Paragraph. After you write the paragraph, use the Story
Editing Chart on page H-1 in the Appendix to make any needed changes
on page 82.

WIN LEVEL II   LESSON 25

CLUSTERING SHEET   NAME_____

TITLE _____

SETTING PARAGRAPH

WHEN

WHO

WHERE

WHAT

FEELINGS

STARTING EVENT

STORY PROBLEM PARAGRAPH

Did-Saw-Heard-Felt-Said-Problem

ACTION-SOLUTION PARAGRAPH

Did-Saw-Heard-Felt-Said-Solution

CONCLUSION PARAGRAPH

Did Next-Learned-Feel

81

WIN LEVEL II   LESSON 25

WRITING A STORY PROBLEM PARAGRAPH
(Continued from page 79)
Name _____

Title

**Setting
Paragraph** ———▶
Tells: When, Who,
Where, What,
Feelings and about
Starting Event.

**Story Problem
Paragraph** ———▶
Tells exciting things
characters Did, Saw,
Heard, Felt and Said
during the Starting
Event. Tells Scary or
Worrisome or Funny
Things about the
Story Problem.

**Action-Solution
Paragraph** ———▶
Tells important
things characters
Did, Saw, Heard, Felt
and Said while
solving Story
Problem.

**Conclusion
Paragraph** ———▶
Tells ending details
about solution: What
Charact. Did Next;
What Charact.
Learned; Brings back
Good Feelings.

(Save this page for use with page 85.)

82

WIN LEVEL II   LESSON 26

LESSON 26
WRITING AN ACTION-SOLUTION PARAGRAPH

Objective: To give students independent practice in writing an Action-Solution Paragraph.

TO THE STUDENT:

Write an Action-Solution Paragraph on the Four-boxed Story Form on page 85, continuing the story that you wrote on pages 79 and 82. Before you begin writing the Action-Solution Paragraph, your teacher will review the parts of this paragraph with you.

To help you organize your ideas for writing this paragraph, write some ideas on the Clustering Sheet on the next page. Then write your Action-Solution Paragraph on page 85. After your write the paragraph, use the Story Editing Chart on page H-1 in the Appendix to make any needed changes on page 85.

WIN LEVEL II   LESSON 26

CLUSTERING SHEET   NAME _____

TITLE _____

SETTING PARAGRAPH

WHEN

WHO

WHERE

WHAT

FEELINGS

STARTING EVENT

STORY PROBLEM PARAGRAPH

Did-Saw-Heard-Felt-Said-Problem

ACTION-SOLUTION PARAGRAPH

Did-Saw-Heard-Felt-Said-Solution

CONCLUSION PARAGRAPH

Did Next-Learned-Feel

84

WIN LEVEL II   LESSON 26

WRITING AN ACTION-SOLUTION PARAGRAPH
(Continued from page 82.)   Name

Title

Setting Paragraph ⟶
Tells: When, Who, Where, What, Feelings and about Starting Event.

Story Problem Paragraph ⟶
Tells exciting things characters Did, Saw, Heard, Felt and Said during the Starting Event. Tells Scary or Worrisome or Funny Things about the Story Problem.

Action-Solution Paragraph ⟶
Tells important things characters Did, Saw, Heard, Felt and Said while solving Story Problem.

Conclusion Paragraph ⟶
Tells ending details about solution: What Charact. Did Next; What Charact. Learned; Brings back Good Feelings.

(Save this page for use with page 88.)

85

WIN LEVEL II   LESSON 27

LESSON 27
WRITING A CONCLUSION PARAGRAPH

Objective: To give students independent practice in writing a Conclusion
Paragraph.

TO THE STUDENT:

Write a Conclusion Paragraph on the Four-boxed Story Form on
page 88, continuing the story that you wrote on pages 79, 82, and 85.
Before you begin writing the Conclusion Paragraph, your teacher will
review the parts of this paragraph with you.

To help you organize your ideas for writing this paragraph, write
some ideas on the Clustering Sheet on the next page. Then write the
Conclusion Paragraph on page 88. After you write the paragraph, use
the Story Editing chart on page H-1 in the Appendix to make any needed
changes on page 88.

WIN LEVEL II   LESSON 27

CLUSTERING SHEET   NAME _____

TITLE _____

SETTING PARAGRAPH

WHEN

WHO

WHERE

WHAT

FEELINGS

STARTING EVENT

STORY PROBLEM PARAGRAPH

Did-Saw-Heard-Felt-Said-Problem

ACTION-SOLUTION PARAGRAPH

Did-Saw-Heard-Felt-Said-Solution

CONCLUSION PARAGRAPH

Did Next-Learned-Feel

WIN LEVEL II   LESSON 27

WRITING A CONCLUSION PARAGRAPH
(Continued from page 85.)   Name _____

Title

**Setting
Paragraph** ———→
Tells: When, Who,
Where, What,
Feelings and about
Starting Event.

**Story Problem
Paragraph** ———→
Tells exciting things
characters Did, Saw,
Heard, Felt and Said
during the Starting
Event. Tells Scary or
Worrisome or Funny
Things about the
Story Problem.

**Action-Solution
Paragraph** ———→
Tells important
things characters
Did, Saw, Heard, Felt
and Said while
solving Story
Problem.

**Conclusion
Paragraph** ———→
Tells ending details
about solution: What
Charact. Did Next;
What Charact.
Learned; Brings back
Good Feelings.

88

WIN LEVEL II   LESSON 28

LESSON 28
STORY WRITING LESSON: AN EXCITING ADVENTURE

Objective: To provide students with an opportunity to practice acquired
writing skills.

TO THE STUDENT:

Today you need to write a story about an exciting adventure you had
(or you may pretend you had). Maybe your adventure is about a time
that you and a friend explored a cave. Maybe your story is about finding a
little puppy or a kitten. Perhaps your story is about a horse or dog that
was unwanted but showed special courage by saving your life or saving
you from serious injury.

Maybe your story tells about an exciting race or game. Or, maybe
you have some other exciting experience that happened to you at the
beach or on a trip, or during a time when you helped somebody who was
in trouble. Or, perhaps you have some other exciting adventure which
you want to write about.

Make your story interesting by including details which help the
reader to better understand your story and to enjoy it more. Be sure to
tell where the story takes place, who it is about, and when it happened.
Describe some of the exciting things that the characters did or saw or
heard during their experiences and describe how they felt.

Tell how any problem or danger in your story was overcome. Also,
tell what you learned from this experience.

Now review the Story Starters on the next page.

89

WIN LEVEL II   LESSON 28

STORY WRITING LESSON: AN EXCITING ADVENTURE
STORY STARTERS

You may want to start your story with one of the Story Starters listed below or you may think of your own starting sentence.

1.   The most exciting time I ever had was the day . . .
2.   One of the most exciting adventures in my life happened at . . .
3.   Early one summer morning I hopped on my bike and headed for the lake when . . .
4.   My exciting adventure started when one day I . . .
5.   This experience will be a time that I will never forget. It all started when . . .

NOTE: Before you begin writing your story read "Story Writing Tips" on the next page.

90

WIN LEVEL II   LESSON 28

STORY WRITING TIPS

Before you begin writing your story on page 93, read the directions below.

1. Use words found in the Special Words Lists (Appendix G) and use your Clustering Sheet ideas to help you write an interesting story.

2. Remember to use proper capitalization and proper punctuation (Appendix C) and to indent each new paragraph.

3. Try to write some compound sentences (Appendix E). If there is conversation in your story, be sure to use quotation marks for direct quotations (Appendix D).

4. Try to begin some of your sentences with Sentence Starters (Appendix E).

5. Use words found in the margin of the Story Form to help you include all of the Story Parts in each main paragraph of your story.

6. Write a complete Rough Draft of your story and then share it with two classmates. Then, make any needed changes on your Rough Draft, and afterwards, give the Rough Draft to the teacher for checking. After the teacher corrects and approves your Rough Draft, write the Final Draft (page 94).

7. Use the Story Editing Chart (Appendix H) to check both the Rough Draft and Final Draft of your story.

8. Now, before you begin writing your Rough Draft on page 93, write some story ideas on the Clustering Sheet on the next page.

91

WIN LEVEL II   LESSON 28

CLUSTERING SHEET   NAME_____

TITLE _____

SETTING PARAGRAPH

WHEN

WHO

WHERE

WHAT

FEELINGS

STARTING EVENT

STORY PROBLEM PARAGRAPH

Did-Saw-Heard-Felt-Said-Problem

ACTION-SOLUTION PARAGRAPH

Did-Saw-Heard-Felt-Said-Solution

CONCLUSION PARAGRAPH

Did Next-Learned-Feel

92

WIN LEVEL II   LESSON 28

Name
(ROUGH DRAFT)
Title

**Setting
Paragraph** ———▶
Tells: When, Who,
Where, What,
Feelings and about
Starting Event.

**Story Problem
Paragraph** ———▶
Tells exciting things
characters Did, Saw,
Heard, Felt and Said
during the Starting
Event. Tells Scary or
Worrisome or Funny
Things about the
Story Problem.

**Action-Solution
Paragraph** ———▶
Tells important
things characters
Did, Saw, Heard, Felt
and Said while
solving Story
Problem.

**Conclusion
Paragraph** ———▶
Tells ending details
about solution: What
Charact. Did Next;
What Charact.
Learned; Brings back
Good Feelings.

WIN LEVEL II   LESSON 28

Name
_____

(FINAL DRAFT)
_____

Title

Setting Paragraph ⟶
Tells: When, Who, Where, What, Feelings and about Starting Event.

Story Problem Paragraph ⟶
Tells exciting things characters Did, Saw, Heard, Felt and Said during the Starting Event. Tells Scary or Worrisome or Funny Things about the Story Problem.

Action-Solution Paragraph ⟶
Tells important things characters Did, Saw, Heard, Felt and Said while solving Story Problem.

Conclusion Paragraph ⟶
Tells ending details about solution: What Charact. Did Next; What Charact. Learned; Brings back Good Feelings.

94

WIN LEVEL II   LESSON 29

LESSON 29
STORIES WITHOUT A PROBLEM BUT WITH A GOAL

Objective: To help students understand the differences between stories
with a Problem and stories with a Goal or Challenge.

TO THE STUDENT:

Thus far, your lessons have been about writing stories **with** a
Problem; however, some stories do not have a Problem. In place of a
Problem, some stories have exciting or interesting situations in which
the characters try to reach a Goal (or they accept a Challenge) they want
very much to reach.

Stories with a Goal or Challenge have many of the same Story Parts
about which you have already learned. However, there are some
differences between stories with a Problem and stories with a Goal or
Challenge. An example of a story with a Goal or Challenge is **Skiing on
Snow Mountain** on page 97. While you are reading this story, please
notice that it has Four Major Paragraphs. These four paragraphs are:

   I.   Setting Paragraph
   II.   Goal Paragraph
   III.   Action-Goal is Reached Paragraph
   IV.   Conclusion Paragraph

Also, notice that **Skiing on Snow Mountain** has special Connecting
Sentences which connect the Four Major Paragraphs. Just like the
connecting Sentences in a story with a Problem, these Connecting
Sentences connect the paragraphs in a logical manner. The Connecting
Sentences in **Skiing on Snow Mountain** on page 97 are in **bold print** and
labeled for easy identification.

95

WIN LEVEL II   LESSON 29

You should be aware that in **Skiing on Snow Mountain** there is **no** Problem at the end of the second paragraph. Instead, the last sentence in the second paragraph tells about a Goal or Challenge. Another important difference between a story with a Problem and a story with a Goal or Challenge is found in the third paragraph of **Skiing on Snow Mountain**. The last sentence of the third paragraph in this story is called the "Goal (or Challenge) is Reached Sentence" instead of the "Solution Sentence."

After you finish reading **Skiing on Snow Mountain**, then read the directions on page 98.

WIN LEVEL II   LESSON 29

Name
_____

Title   **Skiing on Snow Mountain**

**Setting
Paragraph** ——————→ | Early one winter morning, my parents said that |
| they were taking my buddy, Ryan, and me skiing. I |
| jumped up and down with excitement. After getting |
Starting Event | our equipment ready, we picked up Ryan. **We were** |
Sentence ——————→ | **finally on our way to Snow Mountain.** |

**Goal
Paragraph** ——————→ | As the city disappeared behind us, we saw tree- |
| covered mountains. Except for the sound of a big |
| truck once in a while, the countryside was quiet. On |
| the way, Dad stopped to help a lady fix a flat tire. |
| Ryan and I were anxious to get going again. Then we |
| saw Snow Mountain. **It seemed almost too steep for** |
Goal Sentence ——————→ | **skiing.** |

**Action-Goal is
Reached
Paragraph** ——————→ | Just after parking near Snow Mountain Lodge, |
| Ryan and I spied the ski lift. We grabbed our skis and |
| ran for the lift. Mom and Dad yelled, "Have fun," as we |
| hopped on. I felt a little nervous as the lift carried us |
| up the mountain. Near the top we jumped off. Soon we |
| were speeding down the mountain, hearing only the |
| sound of our skis. Near the bottom we hit a small |
| rise. My heart was pounding as Ryan and I sailed into |
**Goal is Reached
Sentence** ——————→ | space. **We finally landed in a heap, dazed but unhurt.** |

**Conclusion
Paragraph** ——————→ | Ryan and I talked excitedly about our "flight" while |
| we were brushing off the snow and heading back to the |
| lodge. Mom and Dad smiled when we told them about |
| our "space flight." **Ryan and I decided that nothing** |
**Future Goal
Sentence** ——————→ | **was more fun than skiing, but we would be more** |
| **careful next time.** |

WIN LEVEL II   LESSON 29

After you have finished reading **Skiing on Snow Mountain**, you should read **The Late Night Fire** found on the next page. While you are reading **The Late Night Fire**, compare the paragraphs of this story and **Skiing on Snow Mountain** so that you might get a better sense of how the two story types (1. with a Problem, 2. with a Goal or Challenge) are alike and how they are different.

When you have finished the above assignment, go to page 100.

98

WIN LEVEL II   LESSON 29

Name

Title   **THE LATE NIGHT FIRE**

Setting
Paragraph ——————▶ | It was very late at night. My parents were gone. I
was home alone. I decided to make some cocoa and a
sandwich. I sat down to watch TV. **Then I heard a**
strange noise.

Starting Event
Sentence ——————▶

Story Problem
Paragraph ——————▶ | I went to the front door to look around. I tried to
figure out where the noise was coming from. It was
getting louder. Suddenly, I saw smoke coming up
behind the barn. The sound of fire roared in my ears.
I rushed back into the house and called the fire department. **When I looked outside again, the crackling fire**
was nearing the barn.

Story Problem
Sentence ——————▶

Action-Solution
Paragraph——————▶ | I raced to the shed and grabbed a hose. Nervously,
I turned on the water. The fire still crept closer to the
barn. Then the sounds of sirens could be heard as
two big fire trucks came roaring up our road. Soon
firemen were spraying tons of water around the barn
and on the fire. The firemen were winnng the battle.

Solution
Sentence——————▶ | **They put out the fire and saved our barn.**

Conclusion
Paragraph ——————▶ | While the firemen were putting away their hoses,
my parents came home. My mom and dad said that I
was a hero. I felt proud. I was thankful the barn was

What Characters
Learned Sentence▶ | saved. **I learned how important firemen can be.**

99

WIN LEVEL II   LESSON 29

SIMILARITIES AND DIFFERENCES BETWEEN STORY TYPES

Shown below in an outline format is a summary of the similiarities and differences between a "Story with a Problem" and a "Story with a Goal or Challenge."

STORY WITH A PROBLEM

STORY WITH A GOAL OR CHALLENGE

Setting Paragraph

Setting Paragraph

Setting Paragraphs have the same parts

Story Problem Paragraph
Characters confronted
with a Problem

Goal Paragraph
Characters confronted
with a Goal or Challenge

Action-Solution Paragraph
Characters work toward
solving Problem

Action-Goal Reached Paragraph
Characters work towards
reaching a Goal or meeting a
Challenge

Conclusion Paragraph
Tells what characters
learned from experience

Conclusion Paragraph
Tells about characters'
future Goal

WIN LEVEL II   LESSON 30

LESSON 30
WRITING A STORY WITH A GOAL

Objective: To provide student with an opportunity to practice writing a story with a Goal or Challenge.

TO THE STUDENT:

Beginning on page 104, write a story with a Goal or a Challenge which the characters want to reach. Possible ideas for a story include: Doing something or making something to earn money, such as putting on a play and needing to sell lots of tickets; making a fantastic clubhouse or treehouse to rent to other kids; making a movie and selling tickets; making a new type of sauce for hot dogs you can sell; printing a neighborhood newspaper or any idea you might have that a character could try to do—even fantasy ideas can work! Another idea could be about trying to win a contest to prove to someone, maybe your parents, that you really are good in a particular sport (horseback riding, swimming, skiing, running, and so forth).

Remember to write a story in which the character or the characters want to reach a Goal, but where no Story Problem happens. Before you begin writing, read the "Story Writing Tips" on the next page.

WIN LEVEL II   LESSON 30

STORY WRITING TIPS

Before you begin writing your story on page 104, read the directions below.

1. Use words found in the Special Words Lists (Appendix G) and use your Clustering Sheet ideas to help you write an interesting story.

2. Remember to use proper capitalization and proper punctuation (Appendix C) and to indent each new paragraph.

3. Try to write some compound sentences (Appendix E). If there is conversation in your story, be sure to use quotation marks for direct quotations (Appendix D).

4. Try to begin some of your sentences with Sentence Starters (Appendix E).

5. Use words found in the margin of the Story Form to help you include all of the Story Parts in each main paragraph of your story.

6. Write a complete Rough Draft of your story and then share it with two classmates. Then, make any needed changes on your Rough Draft, and afterwards, give the Rough Draft to the teacher for checking. After the teacher corrects and approves your Rough Draft, write the Final Draft (page 105).

7. Use the Story Editing Chart (Appendix H) to check both the Rough Draft and Final Draft of your story.

8. Now, before you begin writing your Rough Draft on page 104, write some story ideas on the Clustering Sheet on the next page.

WIN LEVEL II   LESSON 30

CLUSTERING   NAME_____

TITLE _____

SETTING PARAGRAPH

WHEN

WHO

WHERE

WHAT

FEELINGS

STARTING EVENT

GOAL/CHALLENGE PARAGRAPH

Did-Saw-Heard-Felt-Said-Goal

ACTION-GOAL REACHED PARAGRAPH

Did-Saw-Heard-Felt-Said-Goal Reached

CONCLUSION PARAGRAPH

Did Next-Learned-Feel-Future Goal

103

WIN LEVEL II   LESSON 30

(ROUGH DRAFT)
<u>**Story without a Problem, but with a Goal**</u>   Name _____
Title

Setting
Paragraph ——————▶
Tells: When, Who,
Where, What,
Feelings, Starting
Event and Goal.

Goal/Challenge
Paragraph ——————▶
Tells exciting things
characters Did, Saw,
Heard, Felt and Said
while working toward
the Goal and
Finishing the
Starting Event.

Goal Reached
Paragraph ——————▶
Tells important
things characters
Did, Saw, Heard, Felt
and Said to finally
prove the Goal is
reached.

Conclusion
Paragraph ——————▶
Tells what will
happen now that
Goal is reached;
Feeling; and Future
Goal.

104

WIN LEVEL II   LESSON 30

(FINAL DRAFT)
Story without a Problem, but with a Goal   Name _____
Title

Setting
Paragraph ——————▶
Tells: When, Who,
Where, What,
Feelings, Starting
Event and Goal.

Goal/Challenge
Paragraph ——————▶
Tells exciting things
characters Did, Saw,
Heard, Felt and Said
while working toward
the Goal and
Finishing the
Starting Event.

Goal Reached
Paragraph——————▶
Tells important
things characters
Did, Saw, Heard, Felt
and Said to finally
prove the Goal is
reached.

Conclusion
Paragraph ——————▶
Tells what will
happen now that
Goal is reached;
Feeling; and Future
Goal.

105

WIN LEVEL II   LESSON 30

APPENDICES

- A "Working Appendices" for the "Story Writing Teaching" Teacher.

- Materials designed to supplement, extend, and enhance the students' writing experiences.

APPENDIX A
STORY EXPANSION: USING STORY PROBLEM FORMAT

Objective: To provide story models of increasing sophistication
which serve as standards for evaluating students' stories.

The following sequence of four story levels (actually, one story presented in four graduated levels of sophistication) can assist the teacher in showing students how stories develop from the simplest, least exciting level, to the more exciting levels. Starting with the most rudimentary story—but one that is still logically structured—this sequence of levels progresses to stories that excite the imagination and may even make you laugh; yet, these story levels remain logically structured and clearly based on the initial, rudimentary level.

Each level evolves into the next level understandably, smoothly, and logically. Each story also strikingly reveals to students the logical structure of a story and the possibilities for having fun creatively while writing within that structure. This expansion of story levels also illustrates how transitions can be formed between the basic sections of a story.

After students have been introduced to the first level of the Story Expansion sequence—the Single-Star Level—and have become familiar with the four Connecting Sentences (in bold print for easy identification), the teacher may find it beneficial for students to write a few Single-Star Level Stories. This will reinforce for students the logical structure of a story and help them to keep this logical structure in mind as they read the succeeding levels of the Story Expansion sequence. **Note:** These Single-Star Level writing experiences should not be necessary for students who have completed the WIN Level I Program.

Each level in the Story Expansion sequence is prefaced by a section called "Class Discussion Possibilities." This section highlights the most noteworthy characteristics of each level that the teacher may want to discuss with the students. One characteristic of the stories not emphasized in the discussion is the wide variety of sentence types. A brief discussion of this characteristic seemed more appropriate in this introduction. Simply stated, the stories do advance in the complexity of sentence types, including the use of compound sentences, complex sentences, and conversation. Some information and/or practice related to capitalization, punctuation, quotation marks and conversation, clauses and compound sentences can be found in Appendices C, D, and E. The teacher is encouraged to supplement these materials with regular, related classroom lessons.

A-1

WIN LEVEL II   APPENDIX A

Although the Level II WIN Program is designed primarily for third and fourth-grade students, the writing skills of these students may vary greatly. Therefore, the Story Expansion section includes stories at the first and second grade levels as well as the third and fourth grades. The number of stars at the top of each story sample equates to the grade level at which students of that grade would generally be expected to write. In other words, first grade students would be expected to write at least at the Single-Star Level. Most second-graders would be expected to write at the Two-Star Level. The Three-Star Level should be the writing goal for most third grade students. There may be fourth-graders who also should not be expected to achieve above this level. However, the Four-Star Level should be the goal for some fourth grade students as well as, perhaps, some advanced third-graders. **NOTE:** Numbers have been placed in the right hand margin of each of the Story Expansion Models. This has been done so that the teacher can easily direct the students' attention to a specific sentence or passage for the purpose of classroom discussion.

A-2

WIN LEVEL II   APPENDIX A

The Single-Star Level Story—Four "Paragraph" Format
Four Sentences (See Next Page.)

CLASS DISCUSSION POSSIBILITIES

1.   This story progresses logically, but . . .

2.   Each paragraph seems incomplete and to end abruptly due to a lack of
       detail. Compare this level to the Two-Star Level Story.

3.   Transitions between the paragraphs are non-existent due, again, to lack of
       detail. Compare this level to the Two-Star Level Story.

4.   Feelings are omitted. The story focuses on the action only, and hence, the
       story seems "flat" because of a lack of information. Stories that excite us do
       so because they give us action **and** feelings.

       NOTE: Introducing the word "transition" at this point can be desirable.
                     Explaining that a transition is like a word-bridge of information
                     or like details between paragraphs will make discussions about
                     upcoming story levels more meaningful.

A-3

WIN LEVEL II   APPENDIX A

* Level   **THE GREATEST SNOWMAN EVER!**

**Setting
Paragraph** ———————▶ | My sister and I were building a snowman in | **(1)** |
| our backyard. | **(2)** |

**Story Problem
Paragraph** ———————▶ | Our dog came running out of our house and | **(3)** |
| knocked my sister into the snowman. | **(4)** |

**Action-Solution
Paragraph** ———————▶ | We took our dog back to the house. | **(5)** |

**Conclusion
Paragraph** ———————▶ | This time we made sure the door was shut | **(6)** |
| tight so the dog could not get out again. | **(7)** |

A-4

WIN LEVEL II   APPENDIX A

The Single-Star Level Story—Four "Paragraph" Format
Seven Sentences (See Next Page.)

CLASS DISCUSSION POSSIBILITIES

1.   This story is the same as the previous Single-Star Story except that now seven short sentences are used to tell the story instead of four long ones.

2.   This story progresses logically, but has the same shortcomings as the previous story, namely, it is lacking in detail.

3.   However, with seven sentences instead of four, the Connecting Sentences (introduced in Lesson 3) are clearly represented. The Connecting Sentences are in **bold print** in the story on the next page and in other stories in Appendix A for easy identification.

WIN LEVEL II   APPENDIX A

* Level   **THE GREATEST SNOWMAN EVER!**

Setting
Paragraph ———————▶   My sister and I were in our backyard. **We**   **(1)**

Starting Event   **were building a snowman.**   **(2)**
Sentence ————————▶

Story Problem
Paragraph ———————▶   Our dog came running out of our house. **He**   **(3)**

Story Problem   **knocked my sister into the snowman.**   **(4)**
Sentence ————————▶

Action-Solution
Paragraph ———————▶   **We took our dog back to the house.**   **(5)**

Solving Sentence ————▶

Conclusion
Paragraph ———————▶   This time he would not get out. **We made**   **(6)**

What-Was-Learned   **sure the door was shut tight.**   **(7)**
Sentence ————————▶

A-6

WIN LEVEL II   APPENDIX A

The Two-Star Level Story—Four Paragraph Format
(See Next Page.)

CLASS DISCUSSION POSSIBILITIES

1.   The story progresses logically by means of Connecting Sentences.

2.   Greater detail in each paragraph helps the reader to be able to "see" events, and thus, the story is more exciting.

3.   Transitions have begun to form. The words, "We were really mad at Bouncer," form a logical bridge or transition from the Problem ("The snowman got squashed.") to the Solution ("We grabbed his collar and took him back to the house."). Similarly, the words, "We opened the backdoor and sent him in," form a transition from the Solution shown above to What Was Learned ("This time we made sure the door was shut tight.").

4.   Feelings are now evident and enliven the story through the excitement of words such as, "The snowman got squashed," and " . . . the greatest snowman ever."

5.   The Conclusion Paragraph fully satisfies the reader, unlike the Single-Star Level Story, because the unhappiness is resolved. We learn that the characters return and make "the greatest snowman ever."

A-7

WIN LEVEL II   APPENDIX A

✳✳Level   **THE GREATEST SNOWMAN EVER!**

Setting
Paragraph ──────▶ | My sister and I were in our backyard. We | **(1)** |
                       | had piled up lots of snow. **We had almost** | **(2)** |
Starting Event
Sentence ────────▶ | **finished the bottom ball of a huge snowman.** | **(3)** |
                       | | |
                       | | |
                       | | |

Story Problem
Paragraph ──────▶ | Our dog came running out of our house. | **(5)** |
                       | He ran straight to Brandee and jumped on | **(6)** |
                       | her. She crashed into the snowman. **The** | **(7)** |
Story Problem
Sentence ────────▶ | **snowman got squashed!** | **(8)** |
                       | | |
                       | | |
                       | | |
                       | | |

Action-Solution
Paragraph ──────▶ | We were really mad at Bouncer. **We** | **(9)** |
                       | **grabbed his collar and took him back to** | **(10)** |
Solving Sentence ▶ | **the house.** | |
                       | | |
                       | | |

Conclusion
Paragraph ──────▶ | We opened the back door and sent him in. | **(11)** |
What-Was-Learned
Sentence ────────▶ | **This time we made sure the door was shut.** | **(12)** |
                       | Bouncer would not get out again. We went back | **(13)** |
                       | and made the greatest snowman ever! | **(14)** |

A-8

WIN LEVEL II   APPENDIX A

The Three-Star Level Story—Four Paragraph Format
(See Next Page.)

CLASS DISCUSSION POSSIBILITIES

1.   The story progresses logically by means of Connecting Sentences.

2.   Even greater detail occurs than in the Two-Star Level Story, bringing about
      an increased sense of action and excitement. Good transitions are apparent.

3.   For the first time, the Setting Paragraph begins with an action sentence.
      Also, for the first time in a model story level, the reader is given some
      description of the scene: "winter day" and "snowy ground." Ample
      description of the building of the snowman is also provided.

4.   The second paragraph is ready to be divided into two paragraphs as happens
      in the five paragraph format. The first four sentences of the second
      paragraph should be a Starting Event Details Paragraph and the last three
      sentences of the second paragraph should be a Story Problem Paragraph.

5.   Expressive verbs are commonly used in this level: grabbed, yelled, and
      crashing are examples.

6.   In this story model, conversation is about to begin: "We yelled at . . . "; also,
      "We told him . . ." The use of quotation marks is about to begin.

A-9

WIN LEVEL II   APPENDIX A

*** Level (4 Paragraph Form) THE GREATEST SNOWMAN EVER!

Setting Paragraph →

My sister Brandee and I ran into our	(1)
backyard. It was a beautiful winter day. Soft,	(2)
new snow covered the ground. **We were going**	(3)
to make the greatest snowman ever!	(4)

Starting Event Sentence →

Story Problem Paragraph →

We piled up lots of snow to make a tall	(5)
bottom ball. We packed it down and smoothed	(6)
out the sides. Then we made a huge tall belly.	(7)
Already the snowman was taller than we were.	(8)
Suddenly Bouncer, our dog, came running out	(9)
of our house. He ran and jumped on Brandee	(10)
and sent her crashing into the snowman.	(11)
The snowman was squashed!	(12)

Story Problem Sentence →

Action-Solution Paragraph →

We yelled at Bouncer to sit. We were mad.	(13)
Bouncer lay down quietly. We grabbed his	(14)
collar and pulled him back to the house. When	(15)
we opened the back door, Bouncer sat down and	(16)
wouldn't move. **So we lifted him up and pushed**	(17)
him into the house.	(18)

Solving Sentence →

Conclusion Paragraph →

What-Was-Learned Sentence →

We told him firmly to sit and went outside	(19)
again. **This time we made sure the door was**	(20)
shut tight so Bouncer would not escape again.	(21)
Then we went back and made the greatest	(22)
snowman ever!	(23)

A-10

WIN LEVEL II   APPENDIX A

The Four-Star Level Story—Five Section Format
(See Next Page.)

CLASS DISCUSSION POSSIBILITIES

1.   The story has been expanded, including two of the Connecting Sentences,
      but the meaning of the story remains the same. Also, some of the
      Connecting Sentences are not the last sentence in their respective
      paragraphs.

2.   Conversation is used for the first time, giving the reader a "You are there"
      feeling. Conversation also gives the reader a clearer picture of the story
      characters as well as a better understanding of the nature of the sisters'
      relationship.

3.   The story is no longer just four or five basic paragraphs, but is now a five-
      section story. That is, each major story part itself now consists of more
      than one paragraph, and thus, the term "section" replaces the term
      "paragraph."

4.   Repetition of some phrases helps the reader feel more of the emotion of the
      story. Example: "greatest snowman ever."

A-11

WIN LEVEL II   APPENDIX A

**** Level   THE GREATEST SNOWMAN EVER!

Setting
Section ———————→

My sister Brandee and I ran into our	**(1)**
backyard. It had snowed all night and soft	**(2)**
snow covered the ground. The pine trees	**(3)**
looked like white castle towers.	**(4)**
"Let's pile up lots of snow and make a	**(5)**
huge bottom ball," I said to Brandee.	**(6)**
"Yeah, the biggest and tallest we've ever	**(7)**
made!" she replied.	**(8)**
It was a perfect day to make the greatest	**(9)**
snowman ever!	**(10)**

Starting Event
Sentence ———————→

We worked hard and fast, piling up lots	**(11)**
of snow. It did not take long before we had made	**(12)**
the bottom and the belly. Already the snowman	**(13)**
was taller than we were. We packed down the	**(14)**
bottom ball one last time and carefully	**(15)**
smoothed it out. We stopped to admire what	**(16)**
was sure to be our greatest snowman ever.	**(17)**
"We need the ladder so we can make the	**(18)**
head," I said.	**(19)**
"You're right. Let's get it!" Brandee replied.	**(20)**

Story Problem
Section ———————→

Story Problem
Sentences ———————→

(A Connecting
Sentence does not
have to be the last
one in the
paragraph.)

Suddenly, we were startled by the loud bang	**(21)**
of the back door. Bouncer, our dog, came	**(22)**
charging out of our house. With snow spraying	**(23)**
everywhere, **he ran and jumped on Brandee.**	**(24)**
She crashed into the snowman. The belly blew	**(25)**
apart into a billion pieces and Brandee sunk	**(26)**
down into the bottom. Bouncer jumped on	**(27)**
top of her.	**(28)**

A-12

WIN LEVEL II   APPENDIX A

"Bouncer, down! Down!" I yelled.	**(29)**
"Sit, you beast!" shouted Brandee.	**(30)**
Bouncer sat. Brandee got up, grabbed his collar	**(31)**
and pulled him back to the house. I pushed.	**(32)**
When we got to the back door steps,	**(33)**
Bouncer lay down and wouldn't move.	**(34)**
"That's what you think, Bouncer, ol' boy,"	**(35)**
Brandee said firmly.	**(36)**
We lifted him up and pushed him into the	**(37)**
house as his paws scraped across the kitchen	**(38)**
floor. We closed the door and looked out the	**(39)**
window at the greatest snowman ever squashed.	**(40)**

Action-Solution Section ➔

Solving Sentences ➔

Conclusion Section ➔

What-Was-Learned Sentence ➔

"Let's build a new one!" I exclaimed.	**(41)**
"You got it; **but this time, let's make sure**	**(42)**
we shut the door real tight," Brandee suggested.	**(43)**
"You got it!" I replied.	**(44)**

A-13

WIN LEVEL II   APPENDIX B

APPENDIX B

DECISION TIME ANSWERS

Page	Paragraph	Comparative Analysis	Summary
31	Setting	Paragraph 1 is better. The showing, paint-a-picture words "Red, blue, and yellow" in Paragraph 1 excite our senses of sight more than the telling, hazy word "colorful" found in Paragraph 2. Also, the verb "pulled" implies the character's feelings in Paragraph 1 whereas in Paragraph 2 the verb "went" is "flat."	Paragraph 1: Showing vs. Telling Words Exciting vs. Flat verbs Expresses Feelings (implied) vs. Feelings not implied.
46	Story Problem	Paragraph 1 is better. Paragraph 2 uses the telling words "I was scared," but Paragraph 1 shows us fear by using details that imply fear. In Paragraph 1, these details of danger build suspense. Paragraph 2 is missing important information in this sense. Having the pilot fall in Paragraph 1 intensifies the danger and suspense.	Paragraph 1: Showing vs. Telling Words More Expressions of Feelings Greater Suspense More Information
61	Action-Solution	Paragraph 2 is better. Paragraph 2 has sharp details that make us hear and see what the characters are experiencing. This makes for exciting writing: "Roaring flames" vs. "flames;" "white with fear" vs. "scared;" and "rocks were pointed at us vs "rocks were everywhere."	Paragraph 2: Sharp details appeal to the senses
76	Conclusion	Paragraph 2 is better. Compare the first and second sentences of each paragraph. Paragraph 1 uses the telling words "landed" and "glad" whereas Paragraph 2 shows us how the experience of landing felt and excites our senses of sight, hearing, and touch by means of words such as "thump," "crunching," and "basket hitting."	Paragraph 2: Showing vs. Telling Words Better Expression of Feelings

WIN LEVEL II   APPENDIX C

APPENDIX C
CAPITALIZATION AND PUNCTUATION

Objective: To introduce students to the correct usage of capitalization and punctuation in common situations.

This section contains some examples of sentences which illustrate the correct usage of capitalization and punctuation marks
(. , ? !).

CAPITALIZING COMMON WORDS

- **The first word in a sentence** is always capitalized.

  Example: **She** is my best friend.

- **The word "I"** is always capitalized.

  Example: Bob and **I** play soccer.

- **The first word in a direct quotation** is always capitalized.

  Example: Jill said, **"The** pillow is too soft."

  Example: Ryan asked, **"May** I help you?"

  Example: **"Stop** the robber!" the policeman shouted.

WIN LEVEL II   APPENDIX C

CAPITALIZING SPECIAL NAMES

- **Names of people** are capitalized.
    Examples: Ben, Ann, Mary Jones, etc.

- **Names of pets** are capitalized.
    Examples: Spotty, Muffin, Buffy, etc.

- **Names of businesses** are capitalized.
    Examples: Oak Bank, Modern Dress Shop, etc.

- **Names of places** are capitalized (countries, states, lakes,
            rivers, mountains, cities, streets,
  oceans, parks)
    Examples: England, California, Kern River, etc.

- **Title of persons, books, poems, songs, movies, etc.**
    Examples: Dr. Jones, President Johnson, *Star
        Spangled Banner, Robinson Crusoe,*
  Mr. Smith, etc.

- **Names of the days, months, holidays, organizations, etc.**
    Examples: Sunday, Friday, July, Christmas
        Day, Girl Scouts of America, etc.

C-3

WIN LEVEL II   APPENDIX C

COMMON USES OF PUNCTUATION MARKS

Uses of the Period (.)

A period is used at the end of three kinds of sentences:

Statement: I enjoy camping in the mountains.

Request: Please help me carry the box.

Command: Do not play in the street.

Uses of the Comma (,)

A comma is used to separate:

Words in a series: There were boys, girls, men, and
women at the party.

A city and state: Denver, Colorado

A date and year: June 6, 1990

A speaker from a direct quotation: Judy said, "Red is my
favorite color."

Two statements with different ideas: Betty worked very
hard, and soon she saved enough
money to buy a coat.

Use of the Question Mark (?)

A question mark is used at the end of a sentence which asks
about something:

Questions: How old is your car?

C-4

WIN LEVEL II   APPENDIX C

COMMON USES OF PUNCTUATION MARKS

Use of the Exclamation Point (!)

An exclamation mark . . .

is used at the end of a **sentence** which shows **strong feelings**:

Stop the thief!

is used after a **word** which shows **strong feelings**:

Ouch!

Use of Quotation Marks in Conversation (" ")

See Appendix D.

C-5

WIN LEVEL II   APPENDIX D

APPENDIX D
QUOTATION MARKS AND CONVERSATION

Objective: To familiarize students with the use of quotation marks.

    The lessons in this section are designed to teach the use of quotation marks in direct quotations and also to familiarize students with the use of quotation marks in conversation or dialogue.

D-1

WRITING DIRECT QUOTATIONS

A direct quotation sentence has two parts. One part of the direct quotation sentence has the exact words of the person speaking. This part of the sentence is called a **direct quotation**. The direct quotation is enclosed in quotation marks (" ") at the beginning and end of the quotation.

The **other part** of the direct quotation sentence explains **who said the words** in the direct quotation. Sometimes the **speaker**, the person who said the words, comes first in the sentence and sometimes the speaker comes **after** the direct quotation.

Examples:

Bob said, "This is my new bike."

"This is my new bike," Bob said.

NOTE: On the following six pages are lessons which will give you practice in writing sentences with direct quotations.

WIN LEVEL II   APPENDIX D

Name_____

WRITING DIRECT QUOTATIONS
ENDING WITH A PERIOD
Speaker First—Direct Quotation Second

In a sentence with a direct quotation, when the speaker is first and the direct quotation, **in the form of a statement**, is second, the direct quotation ends with a period. Also, **when the speaker is first, a comma separates the speaker from the direct quotation.**

I. **Examples:** Speaker, first—Direct Quotation, second

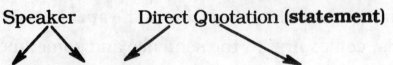

   1. Mary said, "This is a nice picture."
   2. Andy commented, "I like the snow too."
   3. Mark said, "School will begin next week."

II. Write three sentences below, using direct quotations in the form of statements. Write the speaker first and the direct quotation second.

   1._____
   2._____
   3._____

D-3

WIN LEVEL II   APPENDIX D

Name_____

WRITING DIRECT QUOTATIONS
ENDING WITH A PERIOD
Direct Quotation First—Speaker Second

In a sentence with a direct quotation, when the direct quotation is first, **in the form of a statement**, and the speaker is second, **the direct quotation ends with a comma and the sentence ends with a period.**

I. **Examples:** **Direct Quotation, first—Speaker, second**

Direct Quotation (**statement**)   Speaker

1. "This is a nice picture," Mary said.
2. "I like the snow too," Andy commented.
3. "School will begin next week," Mark said.

II. Write three sentences below, using direct quotations in the form of statements. Write the direct quotation first and the speaker second.

Direct Quotation (**statement**)   Speaker

1. _____

2. _____

3. _____

D-4

WIN LEVEL II   APPENDIX D

Name_____

WRITING DIRECT QUOTATIONS
ENDING WITH A QUESTION MARK
Speaker First—Direct Quotation Second

In a sentence with a direct quotation, when the speaker is first and the direct quotation, **in the form of a question**, is second, the direct quotation ends with a question mark. Also, **when the speaker is first, a comma separates the speaker from the direct quotation.**

I.   **Examples:**   **Speaker, first—Direct Quotation, second**

Speaker   Direct Quotation (**question**)

1.   Ben asked, "May I go with you?"
2.   Betty inquired, "Is the bank open today?"
3.   Jeff asked, "Will you help me fix my bike?"

II. Write three sentences below, using direct quotations in the form of questions. Write the speaker first and the direct quotation second.

Speaker   Direct Quotation (**question**)

1. _____

2. _____

3. _____

D-5

WIN LEVEL II   APPENDIX D

Name_____

WRITING DIRECT QUOTATIONS
ENDING WITH A QUESTION MARK
Direct Quotation First—Speaker Second

In a sentence with a direct quotation, when the direct quotation is first, **in the form of a question**, and the speaker is second, the direct quotation ends with a question mark and the sentence ends with a period. Also, **when the question comes first in a "direct quotation" type of sentence, the question mark separates the direct quotation from the speaker**, and **no** comma is needed to separate these two parts.

I. **Examples:**   **Direct Quotation, first—Speaker, second**
Direct Quotation (**question**)   Speaker

1.   "May I go with you?" Ben asked.
2.   "Is the bank open today?" Betty inquired.
3.   "Will you help me fix my bike?" Jeff asked.

II. Write three sentences below, using direct quotations in the form of questions. Write the direct quotation first and the speaker second.
Direct Quotation (**question**)   Speaker

1. _____

2. _____

3. _____

D-6

WIN LEVEL II   APPENDIX D

Name_____

WRITING QUOTATIONS
ENDING WITH AN EXCLAMATION POINT
Speaker First—Direct Quotation Second

In a sentence with a direct quotation, when the speaker is first and the direct quotation, **in the form of an exclamation**, is second, the direct quotation ends with an exclamation point. Also, **when the speaker is first, a comma separates the speaker from the direct quotation.**

I.   **Examples:**   **Speaker, first—Direct Quotation, second**

Speaker   Direct Quotation (**exclamation**)

1.   Amy screamed, "Give the book to me!"
2.   Billy warned, "Stand back from the steep cliff!"
3.   Nancy shouted, "What a great surprise!"

II. Write three sentences below, using direct quotations in the form of an exclamation. Write the speaker first and the direct quotation second.

Speaker   Direct Quotation (**exclamation**)

1._____

2._____

3._____

D-7

WIN LEVEL II   APPENDIX D

Name_____

WRITING DIRECT QUOTATION
ENDING WITH AN EXCLAMATION POINT
Direct Quotation First—Speaker Second

In a sentence with a direct quotation, when the direct quotation is first, **in the form of an exclamation**, and the speaker is second, the direct quotation ends with an exclamation point and the sentence ends with a period. Also, **when the exclamation comes first in a "direct quotation" type of sentence, the exclamation point separates the direct quotation from the speaker** and **no** comma is needed to separate these two parts.

I.   **Examples: Direction Quotation, first—Speaker, second**
     Direct Quotation (**Exclamation**)   Speaker

1.   "Give the book to me!" Amy screamed.
2.   "Stand back from the steep cliff!" Billy warned.
3.   "What a great surprise!" Nancy shouted.

II. Write three sentences below, using direct quotations in the form of exclamation. Write the direct quotation first and the speaker second.

     Direct Quotation (**Exclamation**)   Speaker

1._____

2._____

3._____

D-8

WIN LEVEL II   APPENDIX D

WRITING CONVERSATION WITH DIRECT QUOTATIONS

Whenever you write a **conversation** using the exact words of the persons speaking, use **direct quotation sentences.** Remember, the part of a direct quotation sentence which has the exact words of the person speaking is called a **direct quotation.** Also, remember that a **direct quotation** is enclosed in quotation marks (" ") at the beginning and at the end of the quotation.

The other part of the direct quotation sentence, which explains who said the words in a direct quotation, is **not** enclosed in quotation marks.

Finally, whenever you write a conversation using direct quotation sentences, begin a new paragraph with each change of speaker.

Read the sample paragraph (conversation with direct quotations) below. Then do the assignment on the next page.

Betty said, "I hope that it will be nice at the beach tomorrow."

Judy commented, "If it isn't nice at the beach, then maybe we could go to the park."

"That sounds like a good idea," declared Betty.

D-9

WIN LEVEL II   APPENDIX D

WRITING CONVERSATION WITH DIRECT QUOTATIONS

Write a conversation between two people about a birthday party. Use direct quotations. Remember to begin a new paragraph with each change of speaker. Be sure to indent each paragraph.

WIN LEVEL II   APPENDIX E

APPENDIX E
SENTENCE STARTERS AND COMPOUND SENTENCES

Objective: To give student practice in writing advanced forms of sentences.

The lessons in this section are designed to help students write more interesting and more advanced kinds of sentences.

WIN LEVEL II   APPENDIX E

SENTENCE STARTERS

A **sentence starter** is a group of words, followed by a comma, at the beginning of a sentence that tells either **when, where, how,** or **why**, or tells the **cause** or **reason** something happens. Using sentence starters in your writing adds more variety to your sentences, and therefore can make your story more interesting.

Words which often **introduce** sentence starters include: **When, While, If, Because, After, Though** and verbs which end in "ing" (**Driving, Singing, Doing, Reading, Listening, Playing,** etc.)

Example: **When the show was over,** we went home.
Example: **Standing on the hill,** I could see the ocean.
Example: **If you become lost,** I'll look for you.
Example: **Because the coach was late,** we lost the game.
Example: **While I looked for my wallet,** I found a penny.
Example: **Reading different books,** I discovered many exciting stories.

Now, do the assignment on the next page.

WIN LEVEL II   APPENDIX E

Name_____

SENTENCE STARTERS

Using any of the words in the box below, make up four sentence starters and write them by the numbers below.

> When, After, While, As, If, Because, During, Zooming,
> Walking, Beginning, Trying, Playing, Dashing,
> Hurrying, Shouting, Whispering, Stumbling, Tossing,
> Hiking, Fleeing, Plunging, Declaring

Example: Fleeing with fear, ...

1. _____
2. _____
3. _____
4. _____

Now, using any three of the sentence starters you wrote above, make up three complete sentences below.

1. _____
   _____
2. _____
   _____
3. _____
   _____

E-3

WIN LEVEL II   APPENDIX E

Name_____

SENTENCE STARTERS
MODIFIERS

A sentence starter modifier is a word or group of words which helps to explain or describe the meaning of a noun or pronoun. Modifiers make your sentences more vivid and more interesting.

Example: Feeling happy, Bill rode home on his new bike.

Example: Being curious, Mary began her science experiment.

Using any of the sentence starter modifiers below, make up three sentences and write them on the lines by the numbers. You may want to use words such as **Being, Feeling, Sounding, Looking** as the beginning part of your sentence starter modifier.

thrilled	cheerful	relieved	cranky
furious	shocked	overjoyed	sad

1. _____,_____

_____

2. _____,_____

_____

3. _____,_____

_____

E-4

WIN LEVEL II   APPENDIX E

Name_____

SENTENCE STARTERS
PREPOSITIONAL PHRASES

A prepositional phrase is a group of words starting with a preposition and ending with a noun or pronoun. Prepositional phrases tell why, where, or how something is done. Prepositional phrases can be good sentence starters. They make your sentences more vivid and more interesting.

Example: For two days I enjoyed skiing.

Example: Down the street a fire engine raced.

Using any of the prepositional phrase sentence starters listed below, make up three sentences and write them on the lines by the numbers.

> On the way, Across the river, In the museum,
> Behind the school, Through the door, At the party,
> By the river, Near the forest, Among all the girls

1. _____

   _____

2. _____

   _____

3. _____

   _____

E-5

WIN LEVEL II   APPENDIX E

Name_____

COMPOUND SENTENCES

A compound sentence is two sentences joined together with a conjunction (and, but, or, for, nor, yet) or a semicolon (;).

Example: Bob likes baseball and Mary likes tennis.
Example: She is nice, but he is mean.
Example: Jeff likes soccer; Mary likes swimming.

Write five compound sentences. Use the semicolon in one sentence and four different conjunctions in the other four sentences.

1. _____

   _____

2. _____

   _____

3. _____

   _____

4. _____

   _____

5. _____

   _____

E-6

WIN LEVEL II   APPENDIX E

SUBSTITUTE PHRASES FOR "I Learned"

By substituting for the words **"I learned,"** the writer can avoid overusing them.

EXAMPLES:

1. **Now I know** that I should help you.
2. **From now on** I will be more careful.
3. **In the future** I won't go near the river.
4. **Next time**, I will take my lunch when I go hiking.

WIN LEVEL II   APPENDIX E

SUBSTITUTING FOR THE WORD "Felt"

By substituting for the word "**felt**," the writer can avoid overusing it.

EXAMPLES:

1.   I **was** happy about the party.

2.   We **were** afraid of the lion.

3.   She **has been** concerned about her lost kitten.

NOTE: Words such as "am," "is," and "are" can be used in place of "**feel**" for the present tense.

Example: I **am** sad because we lost the game.

Example: Bob **is** angry because the other team won.

Example: They **are** glad that he wasn't hurt.

WIN LEVEL II   APPENDIX F

APPENDIX F
MODEL STORY CHARTS

Objective: To provide models of Story Writing Charts for classroom use.

The charts in this section are designed to serve as models for the creation of Classroom Wall Charts. These charts are an important part of the "WIN" Program.

F-1

WIN LEVEL II   APPENDIX F

PARTS OF A STORY
SETTING CHART

I. **SETTING PARAGRAPH** - tells . . .

    A.   **When** - the time the story happens.

    B.   **Who** - the characters in the story.

    C.   **Where** - the place the story happens.

    D.   **What** - details which lead to Starting Event.

    E.   **Feelings** - of the characters.

    F.   **Starting Event Sentence** - tells or hints something interesting or exciting that characters are starting to do or is about to happen to them.

WIN LEVEL II   APPENDIX F

STORY PROBLEM CHART

II. **STORY PROBLEM PARAGRAPH** - tells exciting things characters . . .
   A. **Did**
   B. **Saw**
   C. **Heard** → because of Starting Event Sentence.
   D. **Felt**
   E. **Said**
   F. **Story Problem** - tells about the Problem which happens to characters and hints about interesting or exciting things which are going to happen in next paragraph.

WIN LEVEL II   APPENDIX F

ACTION-SOLUTION CHART

III. **ACTION-SOLUTION PARAGRAPH** - tells important things characters . . .

    A. **Did**
    B. **Saw**
    C. **Heard** ⟶ while solving the Story Problem
    D. **Felt**
    E. **Said**
    F. **Solution Sentence** - shows that the story problem has been solved.

WIN LEVEL II   APPENDIX F

CONCLUSION CHART

IV. **CONCLUSION PARAGRAPH** - tells ending details about solution . . .
   A.   **What Characters Did Next.**
   B.   **What Characters Learned.**
   C.   **Brings Back Good Feelings.**

WIN LEVEL II   APPENDIX G

APPENDIX G
SPECIAL WORD LISTS

Objective: To provide synonym lists to be copied for student use.

The pages in this section include five word lists which can help students learn to use synonyms in place of more commonly used words. This section also includes a list which has words related to the senses (Hear, See, Touch, Smell). The authors recommend that each student be provided with a copy of all of the lists in this section.

WIN LEVEL II APPENDIX G

SPECIAL WORDS—LIST 1
WORDS WHICH TELL ABOUT ACTIONS OF CHARACTERS

DID WORDS **SAW WORDS**

walked — walked, strolled, sauntered, plodded, strode, trudged, hiked, ambled, marched, tramped, advanced

threw — threw, hurled, tossed, flung, heaved, pitched, chucked, flipped, lobbed

saw — saw, noticed, gazed, stared, watched, looked, peered, peeked, sighted, observed, spotted

ran — ran, dashed, raced, scampered, scurried, hurried, sprinted, rushed, hustled, scooted, fled, scrambled, hastened, skipped, darted, bolted

fell — fell, stumbled, dropped, toppled, plunged, sprawled, slipped, tumbled, plummeted, dove, tripped

thought — thought, remembered, recalled, wondered

G-2

WIN LEVEL II APPENDIX G

SPECIAL WORDS—LIST 2
WORDS WHICH TELL ABOUT ACTIONS OF CHARACTERS

HEARD WORDS

heard
- heard
- listened
- heeded

SAID WORDS

told
- told
- said
- announced
- declared
- commented
- addressed
- remarked
- explained
- added
- suggested
- stated

complained
- complained
- whined
- grumbled
- warned
- fussed
- griped
- nagged
- moaned
- groaned

SAID WORDS

shouted
- shouted
- yelled
- hollered
- screamed
- shrieked
- exclaimed
- ordered
- commanded

whispered
- whispered
- mumbled
- muttered
- murmured
- stammered
- stuttered

asked
- asked
- questioned
- inquired

answered
- answered
- replied
- responded

WIN LEVEL II   APPENDIX G

SPECIAL WORDS—LIST 3
WORDS WHICH TELL HOW CHARACTERS FELT

FELT WORDS

fear — fear, worried, fearful, scared, terrified, afraid, horrified, frightened, panicked, nervous

upset — upset, irritated, annoyed, aggravated, frustrated, cross, cranky, fussy, restless

anger — anger, mad, angry, furious, upset, enraged, incensed, irate, troubled, uneasy, agitated

uncertain — uncertain, puzzled, disturbed, confused, troubled, bothered, unsure, hesitant, bewildered, baffled

G-4

WIN LEVEL II   APPENDIX G

SPECIAL WORDS—LIST 4
WORDS WHICH TELL HOW CHARACTERS FELT

FELT WORDS

interested —
- interested
- curious
- fascinated
- charmed
- entranced
- amused
- enchanted

surprised —
- surprised
- amazed
- shocked
- astounded
- stunned
- astonished
- awed
- overwhelmed
- dismayed

certain —
- certain
- confident
- sure
- bold
- positive
- assured
- courageous
- fearless

thankful —
- thankful
- grateful
- appreciative
- pleased
- relieved
- gratified
- delighted

G-5

WIN LEVEL II   APPENDIX G

SPECIAL WORDS—LIST 5
WORDS WHICH TELL HOW CHARACTERS FELT

FELT WORDS

happy —
- happy
- glad
- joyful
- thrilled
- overjoyed
- pleased
- delighted
- excited
- eager
- cheerful
- enthused
- merry

sad —
- sad
- unhappy
- glum
- miserable
- tearful
- weepy
- depressed
- sorrowful
- cheerless
- discouraged
- disappointed
- downhearted
- disheartened
- brokenhearted

peace —
- peace
- calm
- satisfied
- contented
- peaceful
- untroubled
- tranquil

sorry —
- sorry
- sorrow
- regret
- distress
- anguish
- apologetic
- remorse
- embarrassed

lonely —
- lonely
- alone
- lonesome
- friendless
- solitary

G-6

WIN LEVEL II   APPENDIX G

SPECIAL WORDS—LIST 6
THE SENSES

Hear	See	Touch	Smell
shouting	shadow	hot	smoke
crying	ghost	cold	ocean air
thunder	footprint	damp	fresh air
voices	fire	slick	pine trees
footsteps	cave	dry	flowers
laughter	passage	rough	food
wind	river	wet	forest
explosion	woods	slimy	clean
barking	trail	soft	fresh
falling object	message	hard	
meowing	stranger	smooth	
moaning	map		
silence	treasure		
cheers	police		
screaming	alien		
whispering	friend		
ocean	diary		
animal			
park			
waves			
pet			

WIN LEVEL II   APPENDIX H

APPENDIX H
STORY EDITING CHART
E D I T S Paper Carefully

E.   **Exciting Paragraphs.**

D.   **Details which describe.**

I.   **Indents Paragraphs.**

T.   **Title of Story.**

S.   **Spelling and Sentences and Sequence are correct.**

P.   **Punctuation is correct.**

C.   **Capitalization is correct.**

H-1

WIN LEVEL II   APPENDIX I

APPENDIX I
STORY FORMS

Objective: To provide students with a variety of story writing forms to
meet specific needs.

Included in this section are a variety of Four-boxed Story Forms for use with
stories with a "Story Problem." Also included is the Four-boxed Story Form for
use with stories which have a "Goal" instead of a "Problem." The use of the forms
in this section will be self-evident. The forms provide students with paragraph
boxes of varying lengths. As the students expand their stories—reflecting greater
skill, more descriptiveness, and increasing complexity—they can use the Story
Forms with longer paragraph boxes.

WIN LEVEL II   **APPENDIX I**

Name
_____

Title
_____

**Setting
Paragraph** ⟶
Tells: When, Who,
Where, What,
Feelings and about
Starting Event.

**Story Problem
Paragraph** ⟶
Tells exciting things
characters Did, Saw,
Heard, Felt and Said
during the Starting
Event. Tells Scary or
Worrisome or Funny
Things about the
Story Problem.

**Action-Solution
Paragraph** ⟶
Tells important
things characters
Did, Saw, Heard, Felt
and Said while
solving Story
Problem.

**Conclusion
Paragraph** ⟶
Tells ending details
about solution: What
Charact. Did Next;
What Charact.
Learned; Brings back
Good Feelings.

I-2

WIN LEVEL II   APPENDIX I

Name

Title

Setting Paragraph ⟶

Story Problem Paragraph ⟶

Action-Solution Paragraph ⟶

Conclusion Paragraph ⟶

I-3

WIN LEVEL II   APPENDIX I

Name

TITLE

**Setting
Section
Tells:** When, Who,
Where, What,
Feelings and about
Starting Event.

**Conversation
adds pizzazz
anywhere in
the story.**

**Story Problem
Section
Tells** Tells Story
Problem with scary
or worrisome or
funny details.

Problem must be
believable and what
causes the problem
must be **believable**.

I-4

WIN LEVEL II   APPENDIX I

**Action-Solution
Section** ———→
Tells important
things
characters Did,
Saw, Hear, Felt,
and Said while
solving Story
Problem.

Solution must
be **believable.**

Suspense:
don't solve
the problem
too soon!
Show Feelings

**Conclusion
Section** ———→
Tells ending
details about
solution: What
Characters Did
Next; What
Characters
Learned; Brings
back Good
Feelings

I-5

WIN LEVEL II   APPENDIX I

Story Without a Problem, But with a Goal   Name _____
Title

Setting Paragraph Tells: When, Who, Where, What Feelings, Starting Event and Goal

Goal Paragraph Tells exciting things characters Did, Saw, Heard, Felt, and Said while working toward the Goal and Finishing the Starting Event.

Action-Goal Reached Paragraph Tells important things characters Did, Saw, Heard, Felt, and Said to finally **prove** the Goal is reached.

Conclusion Paragraph Tells what will happen now that Goal is reached; Feelings; and Future Goal.

I-6

WIN LEVEL II   APPENDIX I

**Setting
Paragraph** ——→

Goal Paragraph ——→

I-7

WIN LEVEL II   APPENDIX I

**Action-Goal
Reached
Paragraph**

**Conclusion
Paragraph**

I-8

WIN LEVEL II   APPENDIX J

APPENDIX J
STORY IDEAS

Objective: To provide students with a wide range of story ideas.

1. Bike race, sled race, boat race, horse race, etc.
2. Roller skating, roller blading
3. Going surfing—surfboarding or body surfing
4. Hot-air balloon ride
5. Going on a ride at an amusement park
6. A camping adventure
7. A backyard sleep-out in a tent
8. Exploring anything unknown—jungle, junkyard, etc.
9. Building a clubhouse
10. Swimming across a lake or river
11. Going to a circus
12. A horseback riding adventure
13. Trapped in an abandoned mine
14. Going rock climbing
15. Capturing an escaped zoo animal
16. Saving a family from a burning building
17. Shipwrecked on a deserted island
18. Deep-sea diving for sunken treasures
19. A faithful dog fights for survival
20. A hang-gliding adventure
21. Discovery of a volcano in Mexico
22. Helping a boy or girl shunned by others
23. A scientist who makes a wonderful discovery
24. Caught in a storm at sea
25. Taming a wild horse for a horse show
26. Adventures of some mischievous kittens

J-1

WIN LEVEL II   APPENDIX K

APPENDIX K
PRE-STORY WRITING OUTLINE

Objective: To provide students with a simplified, first draft story writing format.

The **Pre-Story Writing Outline forms** may be used by students in place of the planning forms found on pages 27, 42, 57, and 71. The Pre-Story Writing Outline forms may also be used in lieu of the Clustering sheet first introduced in Lesson 24. A sample completed story model using the Pre-Story Writing Outline forms as well as a "blank" set of "outline forms" can be found in Appendix K following this introduction.

These forms are designed to enable the teacher to teach story writing to students in a **step-by-step** fashion. However, before the teacher uses the "outline forms" for the first time in place of the pages cited above, he/she should discuss each part (Setting, Problem, Solving the Problem, and Conclusion) of the completed story model ("The Rafting Adventure") just in advance of students writing the part being discussed by the teacher. Discussion of the completed story model can be enhanced by providing copies of the story model to all of the class members or by showing transparencies of the completed model on an overhead projector.

When discussing the parts of the story model (Setting, Problem, Solving the Problem, and Conclusion), the teacher should point that some **sub-parts** of the story are not complete sentences, **but** when combined with other **sub-parts** they form a complete sentence. The Pre-Story Writing Outline forms are organized in distinct sub-parts so that students can focus their attention on one specific idea or concept at a time.

After a student has completed a given "outline form," that form should be corrected/revised (by teacher and student) before the student begins writing the next story part. This practice should be continued for most students through Lesson 27 in this book. When the student has completed the four Pre-Story Writing Outline forms, (K-6, K-7, K-8, and K-9), the teacher may choose to have the student write the final story draft on a four-box form (such as on pages 28, 43, or Appendix I) or on regular writing paper.

Finally, starting no later than Lesson 28 for most students and sooner for some students, the Clustering Sheet should be used in place of the Pre-Story Writing Outline forms for story writing, at least sometimes. The Clustering Sheet is a valuable tool because it gives the students practice in expressing or summarizing important ideas in a few words. Moreover, students may not always have time to write a complete outline draft before doing a final draft.

K-1

WIN LEVEL II   APPENDIX K

Name_____

PRE-STORY WRITING OUTLINE

TITLE: **The Rafting Adventure**

I. **Setting Paragraph** — tells . . .
    A. **When:**   One warm summer day,

    B. **Who:**   my friend, Jason, and I

    C. **Where:**   were going rafting on the rapids at Oak Creek.

    D. **What** characters did to get ready for adventure:
                We got the raft from my garage and carried it to the
                river.

    E. **Feelings** of characters and Why:
                Jason and I were excited about our first time
                rafting.

    F. **Starting Event Sentence:**
                Then we climbed in the raft and began paddling.

K-2

WIN LEVEL II   APPENDIX K

Name_____

PRE-STORY WRITING OUTLINE

II. **Story Problem Paragraph—Because** of what happened in the
Starting Event Sentence, this paragraph tells . . .

Exciting things the Characters:

A.   **Did:**   Looking straight ahead,

B.   **Saw:**   we could see the rapids getting bigger and
                                 bigger.

C.   **Heard:**   The water made a smacking sound splashing
                                 against the rocks.

D.   **Felt** and Why: Jason and I were frightened by the rough
                                 water and jagged rocks.

E.   **Said:**   Suddenly, Jason shouted, "Look out!"

F.   **Story Problem Sentence:**
                                 Then, without warning, we crashed into a big
                                 log and the raft tipped over.

K-3

WIN LEVEL II   APPENDIX K

Name_____

PRE-STORY WRITING OUTLINE

III. **Solving the Problem Paragraph**—tells HOW the Problem is solved by telling . . .

Important and Exciting things Characters:

A. **Did:**   I started swimming towards shore, trying to pull Jason with me.

B. **Saw:**   We spotted some people on the river bank.

C. **Heard:**   They heard our cries for help and jumped in the water.

D. **Felt** and Why: I was glad they saw us because I could not reach the shore.

E. **Said:**   I shouted to Jason that he should not give up.

F. **How Problem Was Solved Sentence:**
                     Soon the people helped us safely to the shore.

K-4

WIN LEVEL II   APPENDIX K

Name_____

PRE-STORY WRITING OUTLINE

IV. **Conclusion Paragraph**—tells . . .

   A. **What Characters Did Next:**

   Afterwards, we rested on the bank for a long time.

   B. **What Characters Learned:**

   I realized that in the future an adult should go rafting with us.

   C. **Good Feelings Characters Have:**

   I felt very lucky that the people on the shore rescued us.

WIN LEVEL II   APPENDIX K

Name _____

Pre-Story Writing Outline

Title: _____

I. **Setting Paragraph** - tells . . .
    A. **When:** _____
        _____

    B. **Who:** _____
        _____

    C. **Where:** _____
        _____

    D. **What** characters did to get ready for adventure:
        _____
        _____

    E. **Feelings** of characters and Why: _____
        _____

    F. **Starting Event Sentence:** _____
        _____
        _____

WIN LEVEL II   APPENDIX K

Name _____

Pre-Story Writing Outline

II. **Story Problem Paragraph** - **Because** of what happened in the Starting Event Sentence, this paragraph tells . . .

Exciting things the Characters:

A. **Did:** _____

_____

B. **Saw:** _____

_____

C. **Heard:** _____

_____

D. **Felt** and Why: _____

_____

E. **Said:** _____

_____

F. **Story Problem Sentence:** _____

_____

_____

K-7

WIN LEVEL II   APPENDIX K

Name _____

Pre-Story Writing Outline

III. **Solving the Problem Paragraph** - tells HOW the Problem is solved by telling . . .

Important and Exciting things Characters:

A. **Did:** _____

_____

B. **Saw:** _____

_____

C. **Heard:** _____

_____

D. **Felt** and Why: _____

_____

E. **Said:** _____

_____

F. **How Problem Was Solved Sentence:** _____

_____

_____

K-8

WIN LEVEL II   APPENDIX K

Name_____

Pre-Story Writing Outline

IV. **Conclusion Paragraph** - tells . . .

A.   **What Characters Did Next:** _____
_____

B.   **What Characters Learned:** _____
_____

C.   **Good Feelings Characters Have:** _____
_____